Micheál's GAA Odyssey

MICHEÁL'S GAA ODYSSEY

A Celebration of Gaelic Games

Micheál Ó Muircheartaigh

with Conor McKeon and Seán Potts

MAINSTREAM
PUBLISHING

EDINBURGH AND LONDON

First published in Great Britain in 2009 by
MAINSTREAM PUBLISHING COMPANY
(EDINBURGH) LTD
7 Albany Street
Edinburgh EH1 3UG

ISBN 9781845965037

All illustrations by Margaret Bourke

A catalogue record for this book is
available from the British Library

Typeset in Requiem and Sabon

Printed in Great Britain by
CPI Mackays of Chatham Ltd, Chatham, ME5 8TD

Do gach éinne a cahbhraigh a bheag nó a mhór le múnlú CLG ó bunaíodh é go dtí an lá inniu.

To those who in diverse ways have contributed to the phenomenon that is the GAA over the past 125 years.

Micheál Ó Muircheartaigh

– PREFACE –

When Iain MacGregor of Mainstream Publishing first spoke to me about this book, I was not overly enthusiastic about the project. He mentioned more than once that he wished it to contain interesting GAA 'trivia'; a discussion then took place on the exact meaning of the noun – almost all definitions linked it to 'unimportance' and thus it seemed difficult to come to any understanding. We then began to talk about the GAA in a general way; before long we were in total agreement that it was a very 'interesting' association in all its aims, attainments, failures, complexities and, betimes, oddities. And yes, there were stories, true or false, and a great deal about events, important dates, teams and, above all, people, so finally we decided that this book would deal with some of the myriad that exist.

The Gaelic Games are all about people and the results of their involvement in the development of a unique organisation that influences life in every parish in the country and far beyond, wherever Irish people gather and communicate. Games of the Gaelic code have now been played officially for over 120 years. Stories from those games live on, as do the factual details about scores, disputes, incidents, personnel, legacies and so on. It is surprising how often they spring up as topics of conversation, especially in the weeks and days leading up to another chapter of matches, even though some may refer to events of generations ago.

In this book, I have thrown forward a few of these as a sort of GAA montage, without the order or symmetry that an architect might demand. They all stem from GAA people, be they 'heroes of great renown', as a ballad might proclaim, or those who contribute greatly away from the glare that thankfully attaches itself to Irish sport. I found it interesting listing these topics, at random I might say, and sometimes came to doubt my own 'certainty' about some matters. Even real experts can easily be thrown off balance when the simple query of 'are you sure?' is directed towards them. On that account, I relied a great deal on Conor McKeon and Seán Potts and I would like to thank them for all their assurances and research when needs arose. *Tá fhios ag an saol gur geal le Seán plé a dhéanamh ar chúrsaí Chumann Lúthchleas Gael agus na daoine a bhaineann leo*, especially the Dublin teams that have given him and others many moments of great entertainment.

Faid saoil chugaibh uilig, and may the day soon come when we see another few counties win the All-Ireland for the first time.

Micheál Ó Muircheartaigh

– CROKE PARK TIMELINE –

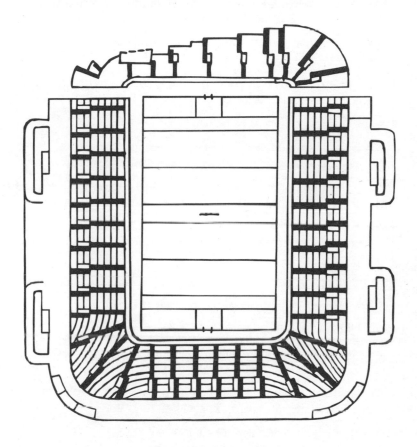

CROKE PARK TODAY

1870s: Site at Jones's Road owned by Maurice Butterly. Used as an athletics course, it is known both as the City and Suburban Racecourse and the Jones's Road Sports Grounds.

1884–1907: GAA becomes one of the most frequent users of the site.

1908: Frank Dineen purchases the 14-acre site for £3,250.

1913: GAA purchases the site from Dineen for £3,500. Ground is renamed Croke Park after GAA patron Archbishop Thomas Croke.

1916: Hill 16 terrace constructed at the 'Railway End' from the rubble of the Sackville Street bombing during the Easter Rising.

1920: Bloody Sunday in Croke Park. Fourteen people, including Tipperary footballer Michael Hogan, are shot in Croke Park on 21 November by the Black and Tans and die from injuries received.

1924: The original Hogan Stand is completed, named after Michael Hogan. Tailteann Games held.

1937: The original Cusack Stand is completed, named after Michael Cusack, founding member of the GAA.

1949: Canal End terrace is constructed.

1952: Nally Stand completed, named after Mayo IRB man and athlete Pat Nally, who strongly influenced the GAA's founding fathers.

1959: New Hogan Stand is opened. Nearly 110,000 turn up in Croke Park for the Pioneer Total Abstinence Association's diamond jubilee.

1961: A crowd of 90,556 gathers at the All-Ireland football final between Offaly and Down – the highest attendance ever recorded at a GAA fixture.

1966: Seating is introduced to the area underneath the Cusack Stand.

1972: Muhammad Ali fights Al 'Blue' Lewis at Croke Park.

1988: Hill 16 redeveloped.

1995: New Cusack Stand completed: first corporate boxes and premium seating introduced to Croke Park.

2001: New stand at Canal End completed, named Davin Stand after Maurice Davin, first president of the GAA.

2002: New Hogan Stand completed.

2003: Opening ceremony of the Special Olympics held at Croke Park.

2005: New Hill 16/Nally Stand end completed and named Dineen Hill 16 after Frank Dineen, who bought the original site on behalf of the GAA.

2007: Rugby and soccer played at Croke Park. First floodlit GAA game played between Dublin and Tyrone.

2009: One hundred and twenty-five-year celebrations marked with fireworks and light show.

– DIMENSIONS OF A GAA PITCH –

GAA pitches used for adult games should be 130 m to 145 m long and between 80 m and 90 m wide. Croke Park is one of Ireland's largest playing surfaces, measuring 144.5 m by 88 m. In front of each goal (6.5 m in width, 2.5 m tall), there are two rectangles drawn out. The small rectangle is 14 m wide and 4.5 m out from the goal line, while the larger of the two is 19 m by 13 m.

There are a series of lines marked across the pitch also. The first, 13 m out from the goal, runs along the edge of the large rectangle. There is also a line running across the playing surface 20 m from either goal line. At 45 m and 65 m (if the pitch is long enough) from each goal, there are further lines drawn from which 45s are taken in football and 65s in hurling. Flags are put into the ground at both ends of these markings on either sideline.

The last marking on the pitch is usually a 10-m-long line right in the centre of the pitch, where the midfielders stand as the referee throws the ball in. Typically, the dimensions of pitches are reduced for underage games, with temporary goals erected on either the 14-m or 20-m lines.

– FREE BOOTS –

The emergence of sponsorship logos on county jerseys in 1991 led to increased demands from the top players for better treatment in terms of free boots, training gear and, subsequently, expenses. However, players' actions often drew them into direct conflict with county board officials. During Down's successful march to All-Ireland football glory in 1991, a dispute arose in the camp during the Ulster Championship when three players, Liam Austin, D.J. Kane and Ross Carr, organised some sponsorship money on the side to buy boots for the Down squad. They were called to task by county board officials before the provincial semi-final and risked suspension for their actions. In their defence, one of the trio pointed out that a third-team soccer player with the local club was entitled to free boots. Down manager Pete McGrath wasn't too happy either as he felt his players should be concentrating on the upcoming match. The players escaped a ban in the end, with the board taking control of subsequent dealings with sponsors and benefactors. However, Austin saw it as a triumph for the players. It was, he explained, 'the first time in 17 years with the county that I got a pair of boots free'.

– GAELIC GAMES: THE FORMATIVE YEARS –

1272 BC: Hurling clash at the Battle of Moytura between the mythical rivals Tuatha Dé Danann and the Firbolgs.

1366: Reference to hurling in Statutes of Kilkenny prohibiting members of the Anglo-Irish ruling classes from playing the game. Also mentioned in Statutes of Galway (1537). Despite the statutes, the game flourishes under early landlords who would organise games between teams of tenants representing different baronies.

1600s: Probable origins of *caid*, the earliest form of Gaelic football. Similar to the beginnings of soccer, where one village would attempt to carry a ball to another while the rival village would attempt to stop them.

1798: Irish Rebellion changes relations between tenants and landlords, Gaelic Games affected as a result.

1840s: Famine has disastrous effect on Gaelic culture; football and hurling in serious decline by mid-nineteenth century.

1884: On 11 October, Clare schoolteacher, athlete and cultural enthusiast Michael Cusack pens an article entitled 'A Word About Irish Athletics' for the *United Irishman* newspaper.

1884: On 1 November, Michael Cusack and Maurice Davin convene a meeting in billiards room of Hayes's Commercial Hotel in Thurles. According to the minutes, Cusack and Davin are joined by John Wyse Power, John McKay, J.K. Bracken, Joseph O'Ryan and Thomas St George McCarthy. (Six others later claimed to have also been present.) The Gaelic Association for the Preservation and Cultivation of Gaelic Games (later the Gaelic Athletic Association) is established, with Davin as president and Cusack as secretary.

1884: In November, the Archbishop of Cashel, Dr Thomas Croke; Michael Davitt, head of the Land League; and Charles Stewart Parnell, leader of the Irish Parliamentary Party, are appointed patrons of the new Association.

1885: In January, new rules are drawn up to regulate sports. GAA clubs are to be formed in every parish. Debate ensues with the Irish Amateur Athletic Association and internal disputes arise.

1887: First-ever football and hurling championships are organised. Teams are 21-a-side.

1888: Tensions grow in the GAA between constitutional and militant nationalists, but the popularity of both hurling and football grow rapidly. The 'Invasion' tour departs for America, playing exhibition matches on the East Coast, but fails to raise funds for the Association. The GAA introduces a ban on the playing of sports organised by rival associations. First All-Ireland hurling and football finals take place between club sides. Referees given whistles and greater power. The size of playing pitches fixed at a minimum of 140 x 84 yd and a maximum of 196 x 140 yd.

1889: Maurice Davin, the first GAA president, resigns after a committee room row over the organisation's finances.

1892: Playing rules are changed, with teams now limited to 17 per side. Goals are given the same value as five points.

1904: First official camogie match played between two Dublin clubs, the Keatings and the Cúchulainns.

1913: In December, the GAA purchases the Jones's Road Sports Grounds from Frank Dineen for £3,500. The ground is renamed Croke Park, in honour of Archbishop Thomas Croke.

1918: On 3 July, the GAA is listed as a banned organisation by the British government.

1920: On 21 November, British forces enter Croke Park during a Dublin v Tipperary football match and open fire on the crowd. Fourteen are shot, including Tipp captain Michael Hogan, in reprisal for the execution of British agents.

1922: First All-Ireland finals contested between county selections.

1922–3: GAA activity affected by the Irish Civil War, particularly in Munster and Connacht. When a truce is called, the GAA helps heal the wounds.

1924: The newly built Hogan Stand is unveiled for the first restaging of the Tailteann Games.

1926: National Leagues in football and hurling introduced into the GAA's intercounty calendar.

1927: Interprovincial championship played for the first time, on St Patrick's Day. The new minor grade for under-18 players is sanctioned by the GAA. At this stage, the modern games settle into an established pattern.

1929: Inaugural minor championships played.

– RING'S RIPOSTE –

The battle between Cork players and the county's administrators has been one of the biggest ongoing GAA stories of the 2000s, but there is a history of tension between players and administrators. Even the legendary Christy Ring had his disagreements with officials. On one occasion, Ring was stopped by an officious steward at a Páirc Uí Chaoimh turnstile. A county board official saw what was happening and intervened. 'Leave that man in. That's Christy Ring, he won eight All-Irelands with Cork,' said the official. Ring replied with a withering riposte: 'And if I wasn't carrying fellas like you, I'd have won another eight.'

– THE UBIQUITOUS PATRIOT –

Pádraig Pearse (1879–1916), revolutionary leader of the 1916 Rising, writer, teacher and GAA official, is the eponymous figure behind several GAA venues and clubs in Ireland and abroad. Here are some of the GAA clubs that have taken his name:

Pádraig Pearses (Roscommon)

Na Piarsaigh (Louth)

Na Piarsaigh (Cork)

Dromid Pearses (Kerry)

Na Piarsaigh (Limerick)

Patrick Pearse's (Antrim)

Annaghmore Pearses (Armagh)

Pearse Óg (Armagh)

Pádraig Pearse's Kilrea (Derry)

Dregish Pearse Óg (Tyrone)

Fintona Pearses (Tyrone)

Galbally Pearses (Tyrone)

Brothers Pearse (London)

Brothers Pearse (Huddersfield)

Padraig Pearse GAA Club (Chicago)

Padraig Pearse Victoria (Australia)

– BORDER CROSSING –

When Maurice Hayes was appointed secretary of the Down County Board in 1956, his target for the county was to win an All-Ireland title within five years. Bearing in mind no team had ever taken the Sam Maguire Cup across the border and that only one Ulster county, Cavan, had ever won the title, it was certainly an ambitious goal. He restructured club football into county leagues and chose a small selection committee to pick the Down team. Down became the first team to wear black shorts and tracksuits, and tactically, they countered the traditional style of football by moving players from their normal positions. It worked. After winning the league in 1960, Down made the breakthrough and won the elusive title against Kerry later that year, adding another two All-Irelands during the rest of the decade, in 1961 and '68.

– THUNDER AND LIGHTNING FINAL –

The All-Ireland hurling final of 1939 between Kilkenny and Cork, which took place in Croke Park on Sunday, 3 September, two days after Germany had invaded Poland, was famous for two reasons: being a cracking contest and the fact that it was played during a violent thunderstorm that erupted shortly after half-time. The storm, accompanied by deafening claps of thunder, frequent lightning and torrential rain, was so intense that fans couldn't make out the identities of the players. The dye from the players' jerseys started to run onto their shorts, while many of the spectators in the crowd of 39,302 scrambled for cover. Reports from the day revealed that the press corps, then situated at the front of the old Cusack Stand, also had to seek shelter.

If the weather was intense, so was the match. Trailing 2–4 to 1–1 at half-time, Cork, captained by subsequent Taoiseach Jack Lynch, fought their way back into the game during the raging storm. Lynch played a leading role for the Rebels, scoring a goal in each half, but while Cork drove at Kilkenny in waves, the Cats had a real hero in defender Paddy Phelan. A fortuitous goal from a Willie Campbell free, which was reported as being flicked to the net by Ted O'Sullivan, left the sides level in the dying minutes, but Jimmy Kelly latched on to a long-range free to grab the winning point for Kilkenny, who finished 2–7 to 3–3 winners.

– DUAL TRIPLE STARS –

Hurlers and footballers are often affiliated to numerous panels during any given season, and there are endless stories of club and county heroes who have displayed extraordinary commitment to several causes and mind-boggling stamina in the process. Dublin's Des Foley, for example, in 1962 became the first player to win Railway Cup hurling and football medals on the same day, while Kilkenny hurling legend Eddie Keher and Joe Keohane of Kerry are the only players to be part of All-Ireland senior and minor final panels in one season. Keher lined out with the Kilkenny minors in the 1959 hurling final, which they lost to Tipp, and came on as a sub on the senior team in the replayed final a month later, scoring two points.

Cork has the most striking record for players committed to both hurling and football, boasting a host of dual stars, such as Jack Lynch, Brian Murphy, Ray Cummins, Denis Coughlan, Jimmy Barry-Murphy and Teddy McCarthy. McCarthy, along with Bill Mackessey, Derry Beckett, Denis Walsh, Teddy O'Brien and Paddy 'Hitler' Healy, have all won All-Ireland senior medals in both codes, but only McCarthy succeeded in winning both in one year (1990). However, pride of place must go to Kerry's Tom Collins from St Brendan's in Ardfert. Collins played in three Munster finals in Fitzgerald Stadium in Killarney on the one day in 1956. After helping the county's junior hurlers to their first provincial hurling success since the previous century, he went on to bag two goals and three points in the Munster junior football final as Kerry ran out winners again. Not spent yet, the irrepressible Tom came on as a substitute in the later stages of the Munster senior football final replay against Cork, although he missed out on the hat-trick of medals as the Rebels prevailed by a point, 1–8 to 1–7.

– LIFE'S A PITCH –

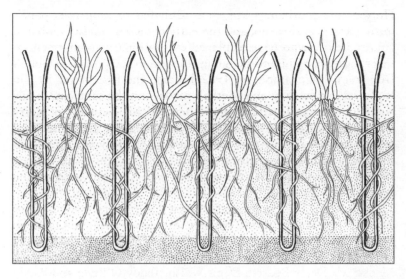

The new pitch in Croke Park was laid in 2002 and has already proved itself to be one of the most durable playing surfaces in the world. In August 2008, torrential rain flooded the area surrounding the stadium two weekends in succession, but the surface stood up to the rigours of the extreme weather and the games were unaffected. The pitch is called a Desso pitch, which takes its title from the pieces of green polypropylene, about 40 cm in length, that are stitched into the surface. These strips are like pieces of nylon string and there are over 86,000 kilometres of them used in the Croker pitch. The string is placed in the ground in a U-shape and grass is then grown around the string, which strengthens the surface and prevents it from being cut up. The pitch is made up of layers of sand, soil, foam, pebbles, geo-textile membrane and plastic. A system of interconnected pipes drains the pitch feeding into two arterial pipes, 600 mm in diameter. These principal pipes are joined to a motor that not only draws moisture from the pitch but also blows air into it, providing oxygen to the roots of the grass.

– ALL THE PRESIDENT'S MEN –

Dublin people are known to be a somewhat indignant bunch and are conscious that their GAA credentials are frequently questioned by their rural colleagues within the Association. Dubliners may have just cause for complaint, too, as there hasn't been a Dublin president of the GAA for over 50 years, despite the density of population in the capital. The last Dublin president to serve was Dr J.J. Stuart (born in Clare) in 1958, when, captained by the legendary Kevin Heffernan, the county's footballers also won the All-Ireland. In total there have been three Dublin presidents. Tipperary and Cork lead the way with four presidents each, although in the case of Tipp, one of their leaders was GAA founder Maurice Davin, who served in the role twice. Kilkenny have had three chiefs, although their first, James Nowlan, was president for twenty years.

PRESIDENTS OF THE GAA

1884: Maurice Davin (Tipperary)
1887: E.M. Bennett (Clare)
1888: Maurice Davin (Tipperary)
1889: Peter J. Kelly (Galway)
1895: Frank B. Dineen (Limerick)
1898: Michael Deering (Cork)
1901: James Nowlan (Kilkenny)
1921: Daniel McCarthy (Dublin)
1924: P.D. Breen (Wexford)
1926: W.P. Clifford (Limerick)
1928: Seán Ryan (Dublin)
1932: Seán McCarthy (Cork)
1935: Robert O'Keeffe (Laois)
1938: Padraig MacNamee (Antrim)
1943: Seamus Gardiner (Tipperary)
1946: Dan O'Rourke (Roscommon)
1949: Michael Kehoe (Wexford)
1952: M.V. O'Donoghue (Waterford)
1955: Seamus MacFerran (Belfast)
1958: Dr J.J. Stuart (Dublin)
1961: Hugh Byrne (Wicklow)
1964: Alf Murray (Armagh)
1967: Séamus Ó Riain (Tipperary)
1970: Pat Fanning (Waterford)
1973: Dr Donal Keenan (Roscommon)
1976: Con Murphy (Cork)
1979: Paddy McFlynn (Down)
1982: Paddy Buggy (Kilkenny)
1985: Dr Mick Loftus (Mayo)
1988: John Dowling (Offaly)
1991: Peter Quinn (Fermanagh)
1994: Jack Boothman (Wicklow)
1997: Joe McDonagh (Galway)
2000: Seán McCague (Monaghan)
2003: Seán Kelly (Kerry)
2006: Nickey Brennan (Kilkenny)
2009: Christy Cooney (Cork)

– THE LABYRINTH –

The GAA's various modern disciplinary bodies can be a source of confusion for the discerning supporter as they track one of their player's fortunes through a mishmash of acronyms. Here we attempt to explain the intercounty system as simply as possible.

STEP 1 – The Central Competitions Control Committee (CCCC):
This group made up of GAA officials is the first step in the process. In most cases, the CCCC will view the referee's report and recommend a set suspension depending on the nature of the offence as reported by the ref. The CCCC also has the power to view video evidence of matches and write to referees and ask that they review an original decision by tape. The CCCC can also decide whether to upgrade an offence.

STEP 2 – The Central Hearings Committee (CHC):
Here, both the alleged offender and the CCCC make their cases to the CHC, whose job it is to impose the recommended suspension, reduce or increase the ban, or clear the player.

STEP 3 – The Central Appeals Committee (CAC):
Once a player is suspended, he can take his case to an appeals board where the CAC will make the decision to: (a) clear the player; (b) reject his appeal; or (c) refer the case back to the CCCC.

STEP 4 – The Dispute Resolution Authority (DRA):
The last avenue of appeal, the DRA is an independent group of people made up of individuals with a legal background and knowledge of the GAA. A sum of money is paid to the DRA, which is generally asked to consider whether a proper procedure had been adhered to or whether there has been some miscarriage of justice along the way.

– PAT O' –

The first radio commentary on a GAA match took place in 1926 when the famous GAA writer and former player P.D. Mehigan broadcast the All-Ireland hurling semi-final between Galway and Kilkenny on the radio station 2RN. Mehigan, born in 1884, lined out with the London hurlers against his native county Cork in the 1902 All-Ireland final and then with Cork in the 1905 final against Kilkenny, and subsequently wrote a regular column in the *Cork Examiner* under the famous pen name 'Carbery'. He also became the first GAA correspondent with the *Irish Times*, where he operated under the pen name 'Pat O". Mehigan was a prolific writer and author of *Carbery's Annual*, which was a must-read item in GAA households between 1939 and 1964. He died in 1965, but his chronicles form a vital part of the documented history of Gaelic Games in Ireland.

– FICTION FIGHTING IN THE GAA –

The first movie of note with a Gaelic Games theme was a short film made in 1955 called *Three Kisses*. Nominated for an Oscar in 1956, the film was produced by the American screenwriter and director Justin Herman (1907–83). It tells the story of a promising young hurler who is catapulted into the big time of success and romance from his humble origins in the small Cork village of 'Ballykilly'. *Three Kisses* was followed shortly afterwards by *Rooney*, a comedy based on a novel by Catherine Cookson. Released in 1958 and directed by George Pollock, *Rooney* features the turbulent life of a dustman and hurler, James Ignatius Rooney, played by actor John Gregson. Gregson was joined by a well-known supporting cast including Noel Purcell, Barry Fitzgerald, Marie Kean and Jack MacGowran. The story charts the rise of Rooney from his lodgings with a family in Rathmines to Croke Park, where he lines out for the Dublin hurlers in an All-Ireland final. Three years after the release of the film, Dublin lost to Tipp in the real 1961 All-Ireland hurling final and haven't appeared in another decider since. Ironically, the Dublin team in *Rooney* is played by the Kilkenny squad of 1957, complete with black-and-amber jerseys.

Similar productions have been thin on the ground since (just like All-Ireland hurling titles in the capital), but it is surprising given the central part the GAA plays in Irish life. Gaelic footballers were briefly depicted in a scene in Neil Jordan's blockbuster biopic *Michael Collins* (1996), but it wasn't until 2001 that RTÉ decided to dramatise GAA life with a series called *On Home Ground*, a drama set in a rural GAA club (Kildoran). The series only ran for two seasons. In 2009, RTÉ began screening an animated children's GAA drama series called *Ballybraddan*.

– PAY FOR PLAY –

Hurling was extremely popular in eighteenth-century Ireland. Landlords organised matches for large sums of money between rival baronies and counties, and while the rules differed greatly from the modern game, the basic elements – hurley, sliotar and goals – were all there. The following is a reference in an eighteenth-century newspaper called *Pue's Occurrences*, to a glamorous intercounty hurling match between Clare and Galway that took place in Gort, Co. Galway, on 16 October 1759:

> There was a grand Hurling Match in the neighbourhood of Gort in the county for a considerable sum of Money between the counties of Galway and Clare; the Hurlers of the latter made a very handsome Appearance. They marched from Gort to the Turlough, two miles distant, preceded by the Band of Musick, a French Horn, a Running Footman and a Fellow in an Antic or Harlequin Dress. None of the hurlers was in the least hurt, the greatest Harmony having subsisted. The County of Clare Hurlers were elegantly entertained at Crushenehaire the Night following and a Hundred Guineas was proposed to be Hurled for, but the Time and Place not yet agreed. The above procession closed with many Carriages and Horsemen, the numerous company at the Turlough made a fine appearance.

– ONE FALL AND YOU'RE OUT –

Gaelic football has had its share of high-profile rows during games over the years, but it would probably have had to deal with far more if it hadn't been for a significant rule change in 1886. During the inaugural year of the new game, wrestling was permitted, with one fall proving decisive. It was an old, pre-GAA custom that players would wrestle with their direct opponents at the end of football or hurling matches as a finale to the day. However, in 1886, wrestling was abolished after complaints that the game was proving too unruly. With teams comprising 21 players a side, wrestling must indeed have been a common feature of Gaelic football in 1885. Those GAA aficionados whose only real interest lies in the 'small ball' might claim that it still is.

– UNDER THE HAMMER –

A laced leather football used during the match between Tipperary and Dublin in Croke Park on Bloody Sunday, 21 November 1920, was sold at a Dublin auction in 2009 for €30,000: more than double the expected price tag. An original ticket for that fateful game, where 14 people including Tipp footballer Michael Hogan were shot by British Auxiliaries, fetched €12,000. A rare All-Ireland football medal from 1943, when Roscommon defeated Cavan, was sold for €20,000 at a 2007 auction, while a set of four medals won by Jim Byrne during Wexford footballers' four-in-a-row between 1915 and 1918 went for €24,000. A medal belonging to Limerick's Malachi O'Brien from the first-ever football final in 1887 between Limerick (Commercials) and Louth (Dundalk Young Irelands) was sold at auction in 2005 for a whopping €30,574. Incidentally, those players who won the All-Ireland in 1887 were not presented with their medals until 1912.

– TEXACO FIRSTS –

Tipperary's All-Ireland-winning captain in 1958, Tony Wall, was the first recipient of the Texaco Hurler of the Year Award. However, the inaugural football award in '58 didn't go to the All-Ireland champions Dublin, who were captained by Kevin Heffernan, but rather to their opponents, Derry, and their inspirational skipper, Jim McKeever. The other Texaco (then Caltex) award recipients in 1958 along with Wall and McKeever were Manchester United player and Irish soccer international Noel Cantwell; golfer Harry Bradshaw, who had won the Canada Cup in Mexico with Christy O'Connor; legendary racehorse trainer Vincent O'Brien; Billy Morton, founder of the athletics stadium in Santry; Irish lawn-tennis champion Eleanor O'Neill, niece of legendary Mayo footballer Paddy Moclair; Irish cyclist and Rás winner Gene Mangan; Irish Olympic runner Bertie Messit; and Olympic boxer Freddie Gilroy. Brazil also won the World Cup that year, introducing a young player called Pelé to the international scene. Still, Christy Ring won the Texaco the following year, a sportsman of rival stature.

– SING WHEN YOU'RE WINNING –

The soccer phenomenon of chanting on the terraces doesn't really exist in the traditional world of Gaelic Games, except for a period during the Dublin football revival of the 1970s when fans on Hill 16 in Croke Park aped those in Old Trafford, Elland Road and Anfield. Even the Liverpool and Celtic anthem of 'You'll Never Walk Alone' was a familiar refrain on the Hill as Brian Mullins, Jimmy Keaveney and David Hickey were going toe-to-toe with Mick O'Dwyer's mighty Kingdom during those epic battles. However, the briefly adopted tradition waned along with Dublin football's fortunes after 1983, and now the Hill's repertoire is pretty much confined to one single ditty: 'Come On Ye Boys in Blue', sung somewhat ironically to the melody of 'Those Were the Days'.

'Those Were the Days' had been released by Mary Hopkin in 1968 after American musician Gene Raskin put English lyrics to the Russian melody 'Dorogoi dlinnoyou', which was written by Russian composer Boris Fomin, who died in 1948. The words were penned by the poet Konstantin Podreviskii, a compatriot of Fomin's, and they deal with the romantic idealism of youth. In the GAA versions of 'Come On Ye Boys in Blue', while the colour is interchangeable for fans of Meath, Kerry and the Republic of Ireland soccer team, nothing really rivals the Dublin fans' rendition.

However, outside of the singing performances of the Dublin supporters, U2, Neil Diamond, Garth Brooks, The Police and so on, Croke Park's most famous vocalist is probably former GAA president and Galway hurler Joe McDonagh, who famously took the microphone after his side had lifted the Liam MacCarthy Cup in 1980, a victory that still resonates today as one of the most romantic stories in modern hurling. McDonagh delivered a rousing and moving rendition of 'The West's Asleep' (often called 'The West's Awake' due to this line in the closing verse: 'But – hark! – some voice like thunder spake: / "The West's awake, the West's awake"'), the patriotic ballad written by nineteenth-century Cork nationalist Thomas Davis.

– RECENT ALL-STARS WHO HAVE NEVER WON AN ALL-IRELAND SENIOR HURLING MEDAL –

1. Joe Quaid (Limerick)
2. Darragh Ryan (Wexford)
3. Ollie Canning (Galway)
4. Eoin Murphy (Waterford)
5. Fergal Hartley (Waterford)
6. Ciaran Carey (Limerick)
7. Tony Browne (Waterford)
8. Mike Houlihan (Limerick)
9. Michael 'Brick' Walsh (Waterford)
10. Kevin Broderick (Galway)
11. Gary Kirby (Limerick)
12. Joe Rabbitte (Galway)
13. Paul Flynn (Waterford)
14. Dan Shanahan (Waterford)
15. Tony Griffin (Clare)

– GERMAN REBELS –

The fractious relationship between Britain and Germany in the run-up to the First World War was often exploited by those engaged in the struggle for Irish independence and, ergo, the GAA. In 1910, the president of the Cork County Board, J.J. Walsh, invited German sailors from a training ship docked in Cobh (or Queenstown as it was then known) to attend a county hurling semi-final between Sarsfields and Redmonds. Hundreds of German sailors rowed up the River Lee and arrived at the game to a rapturous welcome by the local crowd. After the match, spectators flocked to the bank of the Lee to bid farewell to the Germans. As the throng surged forward, a child fell into the river and had to be rescued by a German officer and a rookie sailor, both of whom were later decorated for their bravery by the kaiser. Remarkably, the adventurous Walsh later ran into one of the German heroes while travelling as a passenger on the *Hindenburg* airship over South America in 1935.

– LOW POINTS IN THE GAA –

1891: The GAA's formative years are generally marked by division and conflict, reflecting the instability of the times, but the organisation suffers a serious split following the Parnell Scandal in 1891, which tears Irish politics apart and leads to a decade-long decline in the GAA.

1920: Bloody Sunday. British forces open fire on civilians in Croke Park, including Tipperary footballer Michael Hogan.

1922–3: The Irish Civil War tears the GAA apart, with activity dropping all over the country.

1963: Due to the GAA's 'ban' on foreign sports, Waterford hurler Tom Cheasty is denied the chance to play in a hurling league final because he had attended a dance organised by a soccer club.

1979: The GAA world is plunged into mourning following the sudden death of Christy Ring, one of the greatest hurlers of all time.

1983: All-Ireland football final between Dublin and Galway sees four players, three from Dublin, dismissed by referee John Gough (later christened John 'Off' by Dublin fans) in an ill-tempered affair compounded by the fact that the gates of Hill 16 were breached, leading to crushing on the terrace.

1988: Aidan McAnespie, a member of the Aghaloo Gaelic football club in Tyrone, is shot dead by a British soldier while travelling to a match.

1989: The GAA bans Galway hurler Tony Keady for a year for playing illegally in the United States. Keady, as Texaco Hurler of the Year, is regarded as the top hurler in the game at the time, and the ban is considered by many to have cost his county an All-Ireland title.

1996: All-Ireland football final replay between Mayo and Meath marred by a massive brawl involving the majority of the players on the field.

1998: All-Ireland hurling semi-final replay between Clare and Offaly ends in chaos after referee Jimmy Cooney blows for full-time two minutes early, leading to a sit-in by thousands of Offaly fans whose side had trailed at the time. Game is refixed.

2004: Tyrone captain Cormac McAnallen dies suddenly in his sleep, leaving the GAA community in a state of shock.

– MUSIC TO THEIR EARS –

The whirring sound of a turnstile in full throttle is music to the ears of many a county board treasurer. The man who first introduced this entry mechanism to GAA grounds was J.J. Walsh, who served as a dynamic president of the Cork County Board from 1909 until his Republican activity forced him out of the city. He was subsequently imprisoned. The introduction of turnstiles was only one of several ambitious reforms he introduced to place the board on a business footing, but it had the radical result of increasing gate receipts to unprecedented levels. Walsh went on to serve as Minister for Posts and Telegraphs and, unsurprisingly, as a captain of industry.

– POC FADA –

Tom Murphy from Three Castles in Kilkenny is credited with the record for the longest 'lift and strike' *poc* of a sliotar. He drove the ball a massive 118 m (129 yd) in the old Croke Park at Jones's Road in 1906, a fact recorded in the *Guinness Book of Records*. The annual Poc Fada competition to find the longest striker of the sliotar over a 5-km course in the Cooley Mountains in Co. Louth was introduced in 1961 and takes place on the August Bank Holiday Monday every year. The competition has its roots in the early Irish epic of *Táin Bó Cúailgne* ('the cattle raid of Cooley'), where the tale of Setanta driving his sliotar to Eamain Macha is recounted. The leading Poc Fada specialist of the modern era is former Cork goalkeeper Ger Cunningham, who won the Corn Cuailgne trophy seven times in a row between 1984 and 1990.

– HURLING STRONGHOLDS IN IRELAND –

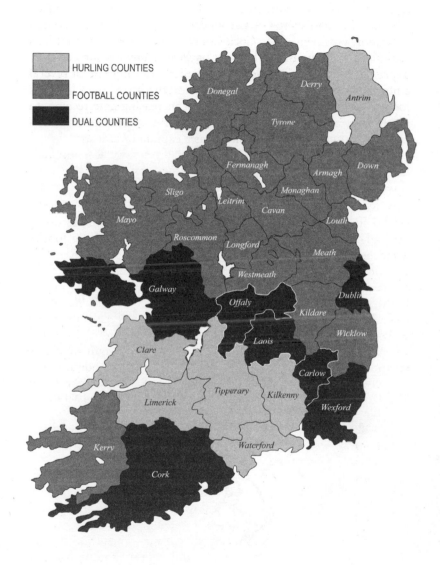

– LEGEND OF THE RING –

While his All-Ireland medal haul may have been equalled, the reputation of Christy Ring as one of the greatest hurlers of all time never will. Ring's premature death aged just 58 robbed the GAA world of his genius, but after his 24 years in the Cork senior jersey, it also ensured that his iconic status was enshrined. To celebrate the GAA's 125th anniversary in 2009, the *Sunday Tribune* listed the 125 most influential people in GAA history. Ring was placed fourth, although, as the highest-ranked player on the list, many would argue that he remains the most important figure in the annals of the GAA.

Ring's unique prowess as a hurler is universally accepted. His record is extraordinary: eight All-Irelands, nine Munster titles, three National Leagues and eighteen Railway Cup medals mark him apart, but even this success fails to do justice to his standing in the game. Courageous, passionate, obsessive, powerful and inspirational, Ring's eccentric, even mystical, outlook on life and hurling only added to his character. He came to prominence for Cork in an era of hurling that was marked by great rivalries and great players. He was ahead of his time in terms of practice and preparation. He was a quiet, religious man who also held deep beliefs about his sport and its unique status in Irish culture. If the history of hurling is based in myth and legend then Ring was the twentieth-century embodiment of everything hurling stood for, real and mythical.

Nicholas Christopher Michael Ring was born on 12 October 1920 in Kilboy, just outside the village of Cloyne, which lies 15 miles to the south-east of Cork city. He was educated at the local school, which he left at 14 to go and train as an apprentice mechanic in the nearby town of Midleton. He then moved to Cork, where he worked delivering oil.

Ring inherited his love of hurling from his father, Nicholas, who would regularly transport him into Cork city by bicycle to watch big hurling matches. He followed in his father's footsteps by hurling with Cloyne as a young teenager, but as there was no minor set-up in the local club at the time, Ring joined the St Enda's club in Midleton, where he won a county minor championship in the late 1930s. By that stage, he had already made an impact in the county and was brought on to the Cork minor panel in 1937 and was a sub on the All-Ireland-winning side that year. The following September, Ring played a central role as Cork minors prevailed again, defeating Dublin in the All-Ireland final.

He graduated to the senior ranks in 1939, making his intercounty debut in a league game against Kilkenny. Cork won the league outright in 1940 and again the following year, when Christy also won his first All-Ireland medal. The championship had to be curtailed in 1941 due to an outbreak of foot-and-mouth disease that resulted in Kilkenny and Tipperary being excluded from the competition. Cork easily defeated Limerick in a rearranged provincial decider before comfortably beating Dublin in the All-Ireland final. Cork went on to win a four-in-a-row between 1941 and '44.

Ring shot to prominence in the classic Munster final saga of 1944 when his last-minute goal secured victory for Cork in a dramatic replay against a Limerick team inspired by the Mackey brothers. This contest has gone down in the history of hurling as one of the greatest of all time.

He joined the Glen Rovers club on Cork's north side in 1941 and won a county medal with them in his first year, the first of 14 county titles, along with a Munster club championship in 1965. He also won a Cork senior football medal in 1954.

Ring's county career lasted until 1963, after which time he had won eight All-Irelands and skippered the team in 1946, '53 and '54. His unrivalled Railway Cup success was achieved during a period in which the interprovincial competition was at its height. He won a Hurler of the Year award in 1959 and a Hall of Fame award in 1971. He was named posthumously at right half-forward on the GAA's Hurling Team of the Century in 1984 and again on the GAA's Team of the Millennium in 2000.

After retiring as a player, Ring served as a selector with the successful Glen Rovers side of the 1970s, but after a brief, unsuccessful stint with Cork, he returned as a selector for Cork's three-in-a-row All-Ireland successes of 1976–8 under Bertie Troy. However, he died suddenly on 2 March 1979.

– BREFFNI BRIEFS –

The fortunes of Cavan's footballers in recent decades may contrast starkly with their historical successes, but it will always be considered a 'traditional' football county nonetheless. From the Polo Grounds final in 1947 to their domination of Ulster football until the mid-'50s, their big-ball tapestry is rich and the county steeped in success. Cavan also have a colourful relationship with All-Ireland finals, and below are seven interesting facts about Cavan's participation in football's September showpiece.

1.   The youngest player ever to play in an All-Ireland final is Cavan's Patsy Lynch, who lined out for the Breffni Boys in the 1928 decider against Kildare at the tender age of 16.

2.   In 1933, Cavan broke the mould for Ulster teams by becoming the first county from the province to win an All-Ireland, with a 2–5 to 1–4 defeat of Galway in Croke Park.

3.   A decade later, in 1943, Joe Stafford inherited the unwanted distinction of becoming the first player ever to be sent off in an All-Ireland, during Cavan's defeat to Roscommon.

4.   A further five years on, in the 1948 decider against Mayo, Cavan became the first team ever to have a penalty awarded against them in an All-Ireland final. Mayo's Padraic Carney successfully despatched the penalty, but Cavan held on for a 4–5 to 4–4 win.

5.   That 1948 All-Ireland success made Cavan the first Ulster team ever to put All-Irelands back to back.

6.   When Cavan beat Meath in 1952 for their last All-Ireland title, brothers Des and Liam Maguire lined out at corner-back and centre-back respectively, while their youngest sibling, Brendan, played midfield for the Royals.

7.   Cavan's haul of five Sam Maguire successes puts them level with Down as Ulster's most successful football county.

– REBEL Cs –

Up until 1919, the Rebel Reds of Cork actually played in a saffron-and-blue jersey with a large 'C' on the front. However, during the War of Independence the British authorities confiscated these jerseys, forcing Cork officials to borrow another set of jerseys, which turned out to be red and white. An All-Ireland victory over Dublin in 1919 in the borrowed strip helped secure the future of the red jersey.

– AN UNLIKELY ALLIANCE –

The GAA has been a cornerstone of modern Irish nationalism since its foundation, so it was with some surprise that GAA fans learned in March 2009 that Glasgow Rangers soccer club was prepared to help promote Gaelic Games in Scotland's largest city. Rangers have an extensive network of community workers across Glasgow, and as part of moves by the club in conjunction with their greatest rivals, Celtic, to stamp out sectarianism, access to Rangers' communities was granted to GAA officers to promote hurling and Gaelic football. The move was the idea of GAA promotion officers in Britain who were working to open up Gaelic Games to a new generation of kids.

The end of the Troubles in the north of Ireland has helped soften the political perception of Gaelic Games, and the Rangers move reflects softening attitudes to the GAA among Protestant and Loyalist communities. The Police Service of Northern Ireland (PSNI), which in 2001 replaced the Royal Ulster Constabulary after the Patten Commission's report was published in 1999, took part in its first official GAA competition in 2007 when they entered a Gaelic football team in the Antrim Inter-Firms League.

In October 2002, the PSNI made history by playing a Garda selection in an unofficial challenge game of Gaelic football, the first such game played after the GAA's removal of the controversial Rule 21, which forbade members of the British security forces from joining the GAA. Since the Good Friday Agreement brought peace and stability to the north, Armagh and Tyrone All-Ireland-winning football teams have been honoured with official receptions at Stormont, once seen as the symbol of the Unionist political establishment in the Six Counties. Democratic Unionist Party minister Edwin Poots spoke at a GAA conference in October 2007 and later made an appearance at a Gaelic football match as the guest of then GAA president Nickey Brennan. However, Poots only agreed to appear at the game after the Irish national anthem had been played.

– STARS OF THE SHOW –

The All-Star Awards were introduced by the GAA in 1971 to honour the top hurlers and footballers of the season. Sponsored by various organisations over the years and with the awards chosen by a panel of journalists, the awards are seen as the next-best thing to winning a medal and provide an annual source of heated debate. The scheme was unrivalled until the creation of the Gaelic Players Association Player of the Year awards in 2006. The inaugural year of the All-Stars was notable for the fact that Cork's Ray Cummins received the accolade in both codes. Kerry footballer Paul Galvin became the 1,000th recipient of an All-Star when he was named on the 2006 team. The Texaco Player of the Year Awards in hurling and football predate all the other award schemes and were first introduced in 1958, when the winners were Derry's Jim McKeever (football) and Tipperary's Tony Wall (hurling). They are also chosen by a panel of journalists.

The first All-Star football team chosen in 1971, a year in which Offaly defeated Galway in the final, was: P.J. Smyth (Galway), Johnny Carey (Mayo), Jack Cosgrove (Galway), Donie O'Sullivan (Kerry), Eugene Mulligan (Offaly), Nicholas Clavin (Offaly), Pat Reynolds (Meath), Liam Sammon (Galway), Willie Bryan (Offaly), Tony McTague (Offaly), Ray Cummins (Cork), Mickey Kearns (Sligo), Andy McCallin (Antrim), Seán O'Neill (Down), Seamus Leydon (Galway).

The first All-Star hurling team chosen in 1971, a year in which Tipperary defeated Kilkenny in the final, was: Damien Martin (Offaly), Tony Maher (Cork), Pat Hartigan (Limerick), Jim Treacy (Kilkenny), Tadhg O'Connor (Tipperary), Mick Roche (Tipperary), Martin Coogan (Kilkenny), Frank Cummins (Kilkenny), John Connolly (Galway), Francis Loughnane (Tipperary), Babs Keating (Tipperary), Eddie Keher (Kilkenny), Mick Bermingham (Dublin), Ray Cummins (Cork), Eamon Cregan (Limerick).

– HANDYGRIPS, TOP-PEGGING AND
TIP IN THE HAT –

Following the foundation of the GAA in 1884, Dr Thomas Croke, Archbishop of Cashel, was invited to become a patron of the new organisation. His influential acceptance letter reflects the nationalist fervour of the cultural revival and the anti-English sentiment abroad at the time. It also makes wonderfully quaint references to archaic Irish pastimes:

> We are daily importing from England, not only her manufactured goods, which we cannot help doing, since she has practically strangled our own manufacturing appliances, but together with her fashions, her accents, her vicious literature, her music, her dances and her manifold mannerisms, her games also and pastimes, to the utter discredit of our own grand national sports and to the sore humiliation, as I believe, of every genuine son and daughter of our old land.
>
> Ball-playing, hurling, football kicking according to Irish rules, 'casting', leaping in various ways, wrestling, handygrips, top-pegging, leapfrog, rounders, tip in the hat and all such favourite exercises and amusements amongst men and boys may now be said not only dead and buried but in several locations to be entirely forgotten and unknown . . . Indeed, if we keep travelling for the next score years in the same direction that we have taken for some time past, condemning the sports that were practised by our forefathers, effacing our national features as though we were ashamed of them, and putting on, with England's stuffs and broadcloths, her masher habits and other effeminate follies as she may recommend, we had better at once and publicly abjure our nationality, clap hands for joy at the sight of the Union Jack and place 'England's bloody red' exultantly above the green.

– WEMBLEY WAY –

One well-known GAA website tried to fool punters with an April Fool joke that the 2009 National Football League final was to be played at Arsenal's Emirates Stadium in London, but while the gag might seem far-fetched to today's Gaelic Games fans, it wasn't so long ago that Wembley Stadium, the bastion of English soccer, was home to an annual GAA tournament. The GAA festival at Wembley was held on Whit Monday between 1958 and 1976, when a series of invitational games were held comprising All-Ireland finalists, league finalists and All-Star selections. The tournament replaced the Monaghan Cup, which had been held annually at the Mitcham Stadium in Surrey, and the Owen Ward Trophy, both competitions that had been run by the GAA in England from the late 1920s to foster interest in the national games among the many Irish in Britain. Over 33,000 spectators turned up in Wembley in 1958 for the first Wembley Tournament games, though the attendance would have been much greater but for a bus strike in London at the time. Kilkenny hammered Clare in the hurling 6–10 to 2–7, while Galway defeated Derry in the football 3–9 to 2–5. Leo O'Neill, a brother of current Aston Villa manager Martin, lined out at right corner-forward for Derry that day, and he played in that year's All-Ireland final against Dublin.

That defeat in Wembley marked the start of an agonising 12 months for the Ulster county, who lost the All-Ireland final to Dublin later in 1958 before going on to lose the league final to Kerry the following year. However, the Wembley Tournament was to remain significant for Ulster. The following year, Down, who had defeated Derry to reach the final in Wembley, went on to beat Galway 3–9 to 4–4, a victory considered by many to be the turning point in the progress of the great Down side. The following year, the Mournemen carried the Sam Maguire across the border for the first time when they defeated Kerry in the 1960 All-Ireland final.

– EARLY BATH –

The 1960 All-Ireland hurling final is famous for the manner in which Wexford destroyed hot favourites Tipperary 2–15 to 0–11, and in particular for the performance of young wing-back John Nolan, who outplayed Tipp's brilliant star Jimmy Doyle. It's also remembered for the fact that a number of Tipperary players mistook a whistled free a minute from time to be the final whistle, and actually left for the dressing-rooms.

– BOARD-GAMES –

GAA board-games have a short history, unlike GAA 'Board' games, which enjoy a long and rather contentious one. However, there is no GAA equivalent to Subbuteo because the use of the hands in hurling and football precludes their mimicry by simple action figures. League Leader is the first board-game endorsed by the GAA and includes football and hurling versions. A board similar to that employed in Monopoly is used and players move around by rolling the dice, while scores are determined by how you interact with the board. The game incorporates all the familiar aspects of Gaelic Games, including rules, terminology and tactics. There is also an Irish-language version of the hurling game.

There have also been a number of electronic GAA games developed for the Sony PlayStation that include the inimitable commentary of *mé féin*. However, unlike their soccer counterparts, the games do not include the names of the players. The most recent addition to this genre is *Bainisteoir Hurling*, a sports strategy game for the PC. As it is endorsed by the Gaelic Players Association, it features the names of individual players. *Bainisteoir Hurling* is a complex game and claims to take players 'on an adventure ride through the turbulent world of intercounty hurling management'.

– WHAT'S IN A NAME? –

Nicknames are common in Gaelic Games, and some of the greatest hurlers and footballers are better known by their monikers. The late Tim Kennelly, Kerry football legend, is one such example in a county where the cognomen is particularly popular. One of the finest defenders of all time and a real anchor man during Mick O'Dwyer's glory years as Kerry football boss, Tim was known affectionately by his fellow players as 'The Horse'. After his teammate Jimmy Deenihan had succeeded in being elected to Dáil Éireann as a Fine Gael TD, Horse Kennelly was present at the count in Tralee and participated in the celebrations after the announcement by lifting Deenihan onto his shoulders. As soon as he had, Kennelly shouted up to the new TD and fellow defender, 'Jesus, Jimmy, I'm carrying you all my life!' The jubilant Deenihan paused momentarily before looking down and replying, 'Tim, that's what horses are for!'

A SELECTION OF WELL-KNOWN GAA NICKNAMES

'Red Collier': Pat Collier, Meath footballer

'Cha': James Fitzpatrick, Kilkenny hurler

'Gorta': Martin Comerford, Kilkenny hurler

'Dodger': D.J. Carey, Kilkenny hurler

'Nudie': Eugene Hughes, Monaghan footballer

'God': Peter Canavan, Tyrone footballer

'Pillar': Paul Caffrey, Dublin manager

'Spike': Michael Fagan, Westmeath footballer

'The Bomber': Eoin Liston, Kerry footballer

'Hands': Paddy O'Brien, Meath footballer

'The Private': Tommy Doyle, Kerry footballer

'Doc': David O'Connor, Wexford hurler

'Shiner': James Brennan, Kilkenny and Dublin hurler

'The Sparrow': Ger O'Loughlin, Clare hurler

'Star': Kieran Donaghy, Kerry footballer

'Bingo': Gene O'Driscoll, Kerry footballer

'Muggsy': Owen Mulligan, Tyrone footballer

'Geezer': Kieran McGeeney, Armagh footballer

'Babs': Michael Keating, Tipperary hurler

'Jinxy': David Beggy, Meath footballer

'Sambo': Terence McNaughton, Antrim hurler

'The Rock': Diarmuid O'Sullivan, Cork hurler

'The Gooch': Colm Cooper, Kerry footballer

'The Pony': Séamus Moynihan, Kerry footballer

'Hell's Kitchen': The entire Tipperary hurling full-back line in the late 1950s and early '60s – Kieran Carey, John Doyle and Michael Maher

'Blue Panther': Anton O'Toole, Dublin footballer

'Goggles': John Joe Doyle, Clare hurler

'Beano': Brian McDonald, Laois footballer

'Gizzy': Diarmuid Lyng, Wexford hurler

'Spider': Jim Kelly, Wexford hurler and footballer

'Bull': Brian Phelan, Waterford hurler

'Fowler': Pat McInerney, Clare and Dublin hurler

'Gunner': Phil Brady, Cavan footballer

'Squires': Bill Gannon, Kildare footballer

'Pook': Tom Dillon, Galway footballer

'Drug': Richard Walsh, Kilkenny hurler

'Gah' and 'Balty': Mick and Paddy Aherne, Cork hurlers

'Hitler': Paddy Healy, Cork footballer and hurler

'Purty', 'Roundy' and ' Lang': John Joe, Tim and Bill Landers, Kerry footballers

– PIPE DREAM –

The 1970s might have been famous for bellbottom trousers, punks and petrol shortages, but it was also the decade that gave rise to a fleeting revolution on the hurling fields. No, there were no surprises in Croke Park during the decade; Cork and Kilkenny both won four All-Irelands each, with Tipp and Limerick bagging the remaining two. No, the revolution came about when Wavin, one of Ireland's largest manufacturers and distributors of plastic pipes and fittings, designed the 'Wavin hurley'. With stocks of native Irish ash on the wane, a synthetic, unbreakable alternative was certainly appealing to the wider hurling community. However, while the product was much trumpeted on arrival, the acid test in the hands of hurlers was an unmitigated disaster and the traditional sceptics had a field day. The plastic hurley lacked any real flexibility and was heavier than the traditional stick. Worse still, when it connected with an opponent's hurley at force it sent a ferocious vibration shooting up the player's arm. While the Wavin hurley couldn't be broken, it also couldn't be used. Galway hurling star Tony Keady famously remarked, 'I used one for a while when I was a kid. It was useless. I got rid of it after one game.' The clash of the ash is still what the market demands.

– PETER THE GREAT –

When Tyrone's Peter Canavan lifted the Sam Maguire Cup in 2003, he shed a tag many observers believed he had inherited for life – the greatest footballer never to win an All-Ireland. The fact that Canavan added another All-Ireland in 2005, steering home the winning goal against Kerry in the final, brought a unique fairytale ending to an extraordinary career in Gaelic football that saw him cement his reputation as one of the most influential players of his generation and one of the greatest of all time. As a finisher, Canavan had few rivals, but his determination, courage and tenacity also marked him apart.

After spending 16 years in a Tyrone senior jersey, Canavan bowed out in 2005 with two senior All-Ireland medals, four Ulster Championship titles, two National Leagues, two All-Ireland under-21 medals and six All-Star awards. He also won six county titles with his club, Errigal Ciarán, and two provincial crowns. He kicked 11 points of his side's total of 0–12 against Dublin in the 1995 All-Ireland decider, the second-highest tally for an All-Ireland final.

Peter Canavan was born into a family of 11 children in 1971 and grew up in Glencull, near Ballygawley. His older brother Pascal was a county teammate for most of the 1990s and they played Sigerson Cup together while studying to be teachers at St Mary's College in Belfast. However, Peter's development as an underage player was somewhat unusual. A local dispute between two clubs claiming to represent the parish meant members of Canavan's club were not properly registered as GAA members, thus forcing the young player to join the Killyclogher Hurling Club so that he would be eligible to play with Tyrone minors. In fact, much of Canavan's progress as a young player was made with his school side.

Whatever the vagaries of his underage career, Canavan quickly made his mark on the county scene, captaining Tyrone to back-to-back under-21 All-Irelands in 1991 and '92. He earned his first All-Star in 1994 after finishing as top scorer in the Ulster Championship. After Tyrone narrowly lost out to Dublin in the 1995 final, Canavan was voted Player of the Year. The following year, Canavan was injured in a bruising semi-final against Meath, but when Tyrone lost at the penultimate stage to Galway in 2001, many believed his chance for redemption had been lost.

However, under the astute handling of manager Mickey Harte, Canavan managed to line out against Armagh in the final despite an ankle injury picked up in the semi-final against Kerry, and was taken off at half-time before re-emerging seven minutes from the end to finish out the game.

His contribution as an impact-sub in 2005 proved equally effective, kicking an incredible winning point from a free in a tense semi-final against Armagh and the crucial goal in the final against Kerry. The pass for the goal in the final was made by Owen Mulligan, a former pupil of Canavan's at Holy Trinity College, Cookstown.

Canavan has always been a leader on and off the field. An outspoken defender of players' rights, he was a founding member of the Gaelic Players Association in 1999. Seen as a Tyrone manager-in-waiting, he also works as a television pundit and writes a regular column with a national newspaper.

– ON THE BOUNCE –

No county has ever won five senior All-Ireland championships in a row in either football or hurling. Wexford were the first county to win four titles in a row in football, between 1915 and 1918. Kerry matched that feat fourteen years later when they won four on the bounce between 1929 and 1932, and repeated it between 1978 and 1981. Poised to make history in the 1982 final against Offaly, Kerry were only minutes from achieving their aim when Offaly staged a dramatic comeback to deny them. Kerry also did three in a row between 1939 and 1941, and again after the setback in 1982 when they returned to win in '84, '85 and '86. Other counties to land the elusive treble were Dublin, who actually achieved it three times during the early years of the GAA, and the great Galway team of the 1960s who won All-Irelands in '64, '65 and '66.

Cork won the first four-in-a-row in hurling between 1941 and '44, but have done three on the trot on three other occasions: 1892–4, 1952–4 and 1976–8. Their greatest rivals, Kilkenny, completed their first three on the trot in 1913, and repeated it between 2006 and 2008, but at the time of going to press, they are seeking to emulate the Rebel County by landing their fourth in a row. Tipperary completed their first three-in-a-row in 1900, and did it again between 1949 and 1951.

– COAT OF ARMS –

Laois won their only senior All-Ireland hurling title in 1915 when the Ballygeehan club represented the county. They defeated Redmonds of Cork in Croke Park to make up for the previous year, when the Kilcotton club of Laois had been beaten in the final. In the wake of that defeat, Laois didn't leave anything to chance in 1915, and after overcoming Offaly, Kilkenny and Dublin to claim the Leinster title, they engaged the services of the famous Dick 'Drug' Walsh from Mooncoin in the run-up to the All-Ireland final on 24 October. Drug Walsh, one of an elite group of players to have captained three All-Ireland winning teams, brought the Kilkenny team to Portlaoise three weekends in a row to help Laois prepare. When the squad travelled to Dublin the night before the game, the Laois mentors kept a close eye on their charges so that there were no shenanigans on the streets of the capital. They togged out in their hotel on Gardiner Street the following morning and walked to Croke Park for the game. Despite all their careful preparations, though, Laois couldn't control the appalling weather that day as torrential rain fell in Dublin. In the end, it suited the bigger Ballygeehan side, who ran out 6–2 to 4–1 winners to claim the county's only senior hurling crown. Incidentally, the whistle used by the referee in that game was owned by the Royal Irish Constabulary.

– EVOLUTION OF THE GAA CREST –

– DEVELOPMENT OF LADIES' FOOTBALL –

Ladies' Gaelic football has been one of the fastest-growing participation sports in Ireland for some years. From humble beginnings, the sport now has an established profile and a presence in every county in Ireland, as well as in the US, Europe and Asia.

1926: Parish ladies' league run in Corraclare, Co. Clare, by Tom Garry of Clonreddin.

1964: First informal tournaments organised in Offaly.

1968: Tournament organised in Dungarvan.

1969: Match organised between Clonmel Post Office and the County Council office in Clonmel. League is organised in the wake of this game, with eight organisations represented.

1970: A number of clubs formed and regular tournaments held during the summer.

1971: Ladies' football convention called in Clonmel in March. South Tipperary fixtures board set up to organise a proper league. Ladies' football championship held in Waterford. County board set up, and on 3 October, Tipp play Waterford outside Clonmel. Challenge games held in Cork.

1973: Divisional championship started in Cork. Cork take on Kerry in intercounty challenge game refereed by Cork All-Ireland star Dinny Long. Kerry travel to Offaly for another challenge. Between club championships and intercounty challenges, the game began to become established.

1974: Several county boards set up. On 18 July, the Ladies Gaelic Football Association is formed in Hayes's hotel, Thurles, 90 years after the founding of the GAA; Jim Kennedy of Tipp is first president. Intercounty championship organised with eight counties taking part: Roscommon, Laois, Offaly, Galway, Kerry, Cork, Waterford and Tipperary. Tipp defeat Offaly in first final. New playing rules drafted.

– ORIGINS OF POPULAR COUNTY NICKNAMES –

ANTRIM: 'Saffrons', from the county colours. Also known as the Glensmen in reference to the striking glens of north Antrim and the area's strong association with hurling.

ARMAGH: 'Orchard County', from the strong apple-growing region to the north-east of Armagh city.

CARLOW: 'Scallion Eaters', from the strong tradition of onion-growing in the county in the nineteenth century. Also known as the 'Barrowsiders', after the river.

CAVAN: 'Breffni County', from the mediaeval kingdom of Bréifne, which was situated in Cavan and Leitrim.

CLARE: 'Banner County', from the huge flags carried at Daniel O'Connell's election-campaign rallies in the Clare constituency in 1828. O'Connell was the leader of the Catholic Emancipation movement in the nineteenth century.

CORK: 'Rebels', originally from the support given to Perkin Warbeck in Cork city in 1495. Warbeck was a pretender to the throne of England during the reign of King Henry VII. The nickname was subsequently reinforced by the county's role in the Irish War of Independence (1919–21) and the Irish Civil War (1922–3).

DERRY: 'Oak-Leaf County', from the county coat of arms, which contains an oak leaf. The Gaelic county name is *Doire*, which means 'oak wood' or 'grove'.

DONEGAL: *Tír Chonaill* or 'Tyrconnell', from the ancient kingdom situated in the north-west of Ulster founded by Conall Gulban in the fifth century. Often used instead of the county's official Gaelic title, *Dún na nGall*, which probably refers to the existence of a Viking fort in the area. Also known as the 'O'Donnell County' in reference to the county's mediaeval lords.

DOWN: 'Mourne County', from the county's majestic Mourne Mountains.

DUBLIN: 'Dubs', an abbreviated form of 'Dubliners'. In recent years, the Dubs has replaced the nickname 'Jackeens' or 'Jacks', which either referred to the mildly pejorative term meaning a 'drunken or dissolute fellow' or to the fact that, historically, Dublin was seen as the most 'English' city in Ireland and thus connected to the Union Jack in various ways. The English word 'Dublin' is a corruption of the Irish *Dubh Linn*.

Fermanagh: 'Erne County', from the predominance of Lough Erne and the River Erne. Also known as 'Maguire County' after the mediaeval lords that once ruled it.

Galway: 'The Tribesmen', from Galway city's title as the 'City of the Tribes', in reference to the 14 merchant families who dominated the town between the mid-thirteenth and nineteenth centuries.

Kerry: 'The Kingdom', from a famous statement made by the orator, lawyer and Irish parliamentarian John Philpot Curran (1750–1817), who supposedly said that the magistrates of Kerry were 'a law unto themselves, a kingdom apart'. In football terms, the latter certainly holds true. But there are many explanations of the origins of the county name. There was a king of the area known as 'Ciar', while *rí* means 'king' in Irish. Another theory – one widely rejected in Kerry – has it that a viceroy came to the palace and reported that an insurrection was sweeping Ireland. When asked was it affecting everywhere, he replied, 'not in Kerry', to which the queen decreed: 'Let's toast the loyal kingdom of Kerry.'

Kildare: 'Lilywhites', from the county colours. Also known historically as the 'Short Grass County' because of the flat, expansive pastureland of the Curragh.

Kilkenny: 'Cats': the exact origin of the name is unknown, although the term 'Kilkenny Cat' seems to refer to anyone who is a headstrong fighter and is based on an old fable about two Kilkenny cats that fought each other until nothing remained but their tails. There are many other stories associated with the name, all of which seem to involve some form of unpleasant activity with cats down through the centuries. The county's colours of black and amber are revered in hurling circles, though their footballers are of the toothless tiger species. Also known as the 'Noresiders' because of the river.

Laois: 'O'Moore County', from the mediaeval clan of O'Moore or Ó Mórdha who inhabited the area and who fought two attempted plantations by English settlers in the sixteenth and seventeenth centuries.

Leitrim: 'Lovely Leitrim', from Larry Cunningham's 1966 hit song 'Lovely Leitrim'. Also known as the 'O'Rourke County', after the clans who dominated the region of western Bréifne. Other terms for the county are the 'Ridge County' and the 'Wild Rose County'.

LIMERICK: 'Shannonsiders', from the River Shannon. Also known as the 'Treaty City' because of the 1691 Treaty of Limerick.

LONGFORD: 'Slashers', from the Slashers GAA club in Longford town. 'Slasher' is a term for a courageous man and refers to Myles 'Slasher' O'Reilly, a seventeenth-century Cavan folk hero. However, 'Slasher' has also been used in a derogatory sense.

LOUTH: 'Wee County', as the smallest county in Ireland.

MAYO: 'Green Above the Red', from the county's colours, which were said to have been inspired by the rebel ballad of the same name written by Thomas Osborne Davis. Other historical monikers include the 'Heather County', the 'Maritime County' and 'Mayo, God Help Us!', the latter referring to the Great Famine and not the travails of the football team.

MEATH: 'Royal County', because the legendary seat of the High Kings of Ireland was situated in Tara, Co. Meath, a county rich in ancient Irish history, archaeology and robust footballers.

MONAGHAN: 'Farney County', from an ancient kingdom of the region that subsequently became a barony in the late sixteenth century. Also known as the 'Drumlin County' in reference to the local topography.

OFFALY: 'The Faithful County': the motto on the county's coat of arms reads *Esto Fidelis*, or 'Be You Faithful'. Referred to as the Faithful County by proud Leinster Council Secretary Martin O'Neill back in the 1940s.

ROSCOMMON: 'The Rossies', abbreviation of the county's name. A less common name is the 'Sheepstealers', after a crime that was frequently carried out in Roscommon because of easy access to neighbouring counties across the River Shannon.

SLIGO: 'Yeats County': though he was born in Dublin, Sligo was the spiritual home of poet William Butler Yeats. He died in France, but his remains were later re-interred, according to his wishes, 'under bare Ben Bulben's head' in Drumcliff churchyard, Co. Sligo.

TIPPERARY: 'Premier County', a title given to the county by revolutionary Irish writer Thomas Davis, although the name could have originated in relation to Tipp's prosperous farmland. The 'Stone Throwers' is an older name and refers to the county's militant agitators during the nineteenth-century land wars.

TYRONE: 'Red Hand County', from the symbol on the GAA county crest, which is the Red Hand of Ulster, also on the coat of arms of the O'Neill clan who once dominated the region. Also known as the 'O'Neill County'.

WATERFORD: 'The Déise', from ancient classes of people called Déisi. Déisi Muman was one such sept that existed in Munster. Also known as the 'Suirsiders', from the River Suir.

WESTMEATH: 'Lake County', from the many prominent loughs in the county including Ree, Lene, Derravaragh, Owel and Ennell.

WEXFORD: 'Yellow Bellies', attributed to a Wexford hurling team led by Sir Caesar Colclough that competed in a game in Cornwall during the reign of William of Orange. Their yellow sashes were worn as a mark of respect to King Billy. This historical nickname is reflected in the existing jersey. Also known as the 'Model County' after the county's model farms and 'Slaneysiders' after the River Slaney.

WICKLOW: 'Garden County' in reference to either the many stately gardens in the county or the proximity of its stunning scenery next to the city of Dublin.

– FLAGS OF CONVENIENCE –

The use of flags by linesmen and umpires goes back to the early years of the GAA. In 1895, ten years after the original rules of hurling and football had been drafted by Maurice Davin, linesmen were permitted to use flags to signal sideline balls and to draw the attention of the referee. The following year, in 1896, umpires began using coloured flags to indicate scores, with a green flag used for a goal and a white flag used for a point. Besides a whistle and a notebook, the GAA referee's equipment didn't change much for a century until 1999, when yellow and red cards were brought into Gaelic Games to indicate bookings and dismissals. Then in the summer of 2004, following a trial period the previous year, intercounty referees were officially wired with microphones and earplugs to communicate with their linesmen during championship games. Despite these advances, disputes over refereeing decisions and rules controversies are as frequent today as at any time in the Association's history.

– HIGH ROLLERS –

When Galway scored 2–13 in the 1973 All-Ireland football final, they could have been forgiven for feeling hard done-by travelling back across the Shannon without the Sam Maguire Cup because the Tribesmen's tally was the highest losing score ever recorded in the football decider. Unfortunately for Galway, high-flying Cork racked up an impressive 3–17 (they were on a roll after bagging 5–10 in the semi-final against Tyrone, 5–12 against Kerry in the Munster final and 2–14 against Clare in their provincial semi). However, the biggest score ever notched up in an All-Ireland football final is a record shared, unsurprisingly, by Kerry and Dublin. The Dubs held the honour after 1977 by scoring 5–12 against Armagh until the Kingdom replied in the 2006 final with 4–15 against Mayo.

– GAA GENERALS –

There have been 18 *ard stiúrthóirí*, or general secretaries, of the GAA since its foundation in 1884, with founder Michael Cusack serving as the first secretary. The turbulence of the formative years of the GAA is reflected in the turnover of secretaries and the fact that there were often overlapping officers. However, this is in contrast to the subsequent conservative nature of the established Association in that from 1900 to the present day, in total there have only been six *ard stiúrthóirí*, and of those, only four since 1929.

The longest-serving secretary was Pádraic Ó Caoimh from 1929 to '64, a Roscommon native but associated with Cork GAA, and after whom Páirc Uí Chaoimh is named. He oversaw the completion of the Cusack Stand (1937) and the new Hogan Stand (1959), so he shares a lot in common with the second-longest-serving secretary, Liam Mulvihill from Longord, who served from 1979 to 2008 and is credited with supervising the redevelopment of Croke Park. Like many GAA administrators, and indeed his successor as *ard stiúrthóirí*, Paraic Duffy, Mulvihill was a school-teacher before taking up his position in Croke Park. He also played county football for Longford at all grades. As well as the significant redevelopment of the GAA's headquarters during his tenure, Mulvihill oversaw a period of rapid modernisation and commercialisation in the organisation, with the growth of live television for intercounty games, infrastructural development nationwide, the introduction of sponsorship and the opening of Croke Park to soccer and rugby. He is also recognised for his contribution to the GAA during the Troubles in the Six Counties, a period of immense strain for GAA members in the north.

GAA GENERAL SECRETARIES AND DIRECTOR GENERALS

1884–6: Michael Cusack (Clare)

1884–6: John McKay (Antrim/Cork)

1884–7: John Wyse Power (Waterford/Kildare)

1886–7: J.B. O'Reilly (Waterford/Dublin)

1885–9: Timothy O'Riordan (Kerry/Cork)

1887–8: James Moore (Louth)

1888: William Prendergast (Tipperary)

1889–90: P.R. Cleary (Limerick)

1890–1: Maurice Moynihan (Kerry)

1891–4: Patrick Tobin (Dublin)

1894–5: David Walsh (Cork)

1895–8: Richard T.C. Blake (Meath)

1898–1901: Frank B. Dineen (Limerick)

1901–29: Luke J. O'Toole (Wicklow/Dublin)

1929–64: Pádraig Ó Caoimh (Cork)

1964–79: Seán Ó Síocháin (Cork)

1979–2008: Liam Mulvihill (Longford) – first 'director general'

2008 to present: Paraic Duffy (Monaghan)

– CENTURIES AND MILLENNIA –

The GAA's centenary celebrations in 1984 were marked by the selection of centenary teams. A nationwide poll was first carried out by the *Sunday Independent* and the results were then considered by a selection panel to produce a 'Team of the Century' for both football and hurling. Fifteen years later, the GAA, in conjunction with An Post, announced two 'Teams of the Millennium', which were selected by a panel of journalists and former GAA presidents. As with most historical selections, the age profile of the selectors is largely reflected in some of the choices. There are few differences in the selections between the centenary and the millennium teams despite the extra 15 years of action. The absence of Kerry's Jack O'Shea in midfield caused quite a stir on the millennium football team, while Dublin supporters were up in arms that local legend Brian Mullins was also ignored. In hurling, there was also a furore that Kilkenny's D.J. Carey was overlooked.

GAA FOOTBALL 'TEAM OF THE CENTURY'

Dan O'Keeffe (Kerry), Enda Colleran (Galway), Paddy O'Brien (Meath), Seán Flanagan (Mayo), Seán Murphy (Kerry), John Joe Reilly (Cavan), Stephen White (Louth), Mick O'Connell (Kerry), Jack O'Shea (Kerry), Seán O'Neill (Down), Seán Purcell (Galway), Pat Spillane (Kerry), Mike Sheehy (Kerry), Tom Langan (Mayo), Kevin Heffernan (Dublin).

GAA HURLING 'TEAM OF THE CENTURY'

Tony Reddan (Tipperary), Bobby Rackard (Wexford), Nick O'Donnell (Wexford), John Doyle (Tipperary), Jimmy Finn (Tipperary), John Keane (Waterford), Paddy Phelan (Kilkenny), Lory Meagher (Kilkenny), Jack Lynch (Cork), Christy Ring (Cork), Mick Mackey (Limerick), Jim Langton (Kilkenny), Jimmy Doyle (Tipperary), Nicky Rackard (Wexford), Eddie Keher (Kilkenny).

GAA FOOTBALL 'TEAM OF THE MILLENNIUM'

Dan O'Keeffe (Kerry), Enda Colleran (Galway), Joe Keohane (Kerry), Seán Flanagan (Mayo), Seán Murphy (Kerry), John Joe O'Reilly (Cavan), Martin O'Connell (Meath), Mick O'Connell (Kerry), Tommy Murphy (Laois), Seán O'Neill (Down), Seán Purcell (Galway), Pat Spillane (Kerry), Mikey Sheehy (Kerry), Tom Langan (Mayo), Kevin Heffernan (Dublin).

GAA HURLING 'TEAM OF THE MILLENNIUM'

Tony Reddan (Tipperary), John Doyle (Tipperary), Nick O'Donnell (Wexford), Bobby Rackard (Wexford), Paddy Phelan (Kilkenny), John Keane (Waterford), Brian Whelahan (Offaly), Jack Lynch (Cork), Lory Meagher (Kilkenny), Christy Ring (Cork), Mick Mackey (Limerick), Jim Langton (Kilkenny), Eddie Keher (Kilkenny), Ray Cummins (Cork), Jimmy Doyle (Tipperary).

– SUBSTITUTE ALL-IRELAND –

The early years of the GAA were notable for frequent disputes. The All-Ireland hurling final of 1911 was a case in point. A strong Limerick side captained by the formidable John 'Tyler' Mackey were to meet Kilkenny at the Cork Athletic Grounds. However, heavy rain left the pitch in a poor state and referee Tom Kenny, along with GAA Central Council officials, deemed it unplayable. Limerick kicked up and refused to switch to Thurles, the suggested alternative, so the game was awarded to Kilkenny. Without a final, the GAA arranged an alternative challenge match between the Cats and Tipperary in Dungarvan, and even had medals struck for the occasion. Kilkenny, sporting their new black-and-amber jerseys donated by John F. Drennan of Conway Hall, won the substitute All-Ireland, the first in a three-in-a-row.

– THE POLO GROUNDS FINAL –

The All-Ireland final of 1947 remains the only major GAA intercounty final to be played outside Ireland. The Sam Maguire Cup decider between Cavan and Kerry was the fruit of the long labours of New York GAA members to host the game and give expats the opportunity to watch one of the Association's showpiece events.

For years, the GAA Congress had rejected the push to stage the football final away from Croke Park, and 1947 looked no different until a letter from an exiled priest pleading for the game to be brought to New York was read by Canon Hamilton to delegates before the vote. Visibly moved by the document, delegates passed the motion – although it later transpired that the letter had been a hoax! And it is even alleged that Hamilton himself had written the letter.

Either way, the decision was never reversed and the game went ahead in the Polo Grounds, then the home of the New York Giants baseball team. Kerry elected to take the long route to the Big Apple, travelling the arduous 3,000-mile journey by boat across the Atlantic while their opponents, Cavan, elected for the more convenient and swift aeroplane trip, though even that took almost 36 hours.

The teams met on 14 September 1947 on a swelteringly hot day in New York, when 34,941 spectators – mostly of Irish lineage – turned up for the historic final. Kerry players, worried about the intense heat in the ground, took to the field in white hats to negate the blistering sun. Champions and favourites Kerry grabbed a commanding eight-point lead before the Breffni men edged their way back into proceedings, and big performances from captain John Joe O'Reilly, along with Mick Higgins and Simon Deignan (who, incidentally, had refereed Kerry's Munster final triumph over Cork earlier that year), saw the Ulster champions prevail 2–11 to 2–7.

The game was also famous for the live radio commentary of the legendary Radio Éireann broadcaster Michael O'Hehir. The broadcast lines had been booked and paid for until 5 p.m. New York time, half an hour after the scheduled time for the final whistle. However, the game was delayed due to the elaborate presentation of dignitaries to the players and the crowd before the throw-in. With ten minutes remaining in the game, O'Hehir realised there were only five minutes left on the 'meter', so he pleaded, on air, to whatever operative might be listening, for 'five more minutes' to give listeners back in Ireland the chance to hear the full game – which they did.

To commemorate the fiftieth anniversary of this unique occasion, the GAA hosted another meeting of the two sides in New York in 1997. Kerry, then All-Ireland champions and managed by Páidí Ó Sé, and Cavan, who had just bridged a 28-year gap under Martin McHugh's stewardship to win an Ulster title, went head to head again, this time in a National League Division 1 match in Downing Stadium. City mayor Rudolph Giuliani threw the ball in and Kerry duly gained some modicum of revenge, thanks to a masterclass from that season's Player of the Year, Maurice Fitzgerald. By the way, the Sam Maguire Cup was not taken to New York and there is no account of where or when it was presented to the Cavan captain, John Joe O'Reilly.

– HURLING AND SHINTY –

Ireland and Scotland share a rich Gaelic culture, and this is reflected in the similarities between hurling and shinty, the latter a game traditionally played in the Scottish Highlands. The Scots Gaelic word for shinty is *camanachd*, or *iomain* in modern Scots Gaelic, almost identical to *camán* ('hurley') or *iománaíocht* ('hurling') in modern Irish – all deriving from the Gaelic word *cam* (Gaelic word for 'hook' or 'bend'). A game similar to hurling known as *cammag* was also played on the Isle of Man.

Unlike hurling, the shinty stick has no bas or blade. An early form of hurling played in the northern part of Ireland, *camánacht*, closely resembled shinty. However, while sharing numerous similarities with hurling, shinty has many distinctive features and rules. A team consists of 12 players, including a goalkeeper, who is the only player allowed to handle the ball. Matches consist of two forty-five-minute halves. The shinty pitch is marked differently from the Gaelic pitch, and free situations consist of penalties, goal hits, shys and corners. Similar to hurling, the ball can be struck in the air and with both sides of the *camán*. A player can also block and tackle with the stick, although coming down on an opponent's stick – 'chopping' in hurling, or 'hacking' in shinty – is similarly illegal. Players can use the shoulder charge as in hurling or football.

In recognition of the shared heritage, an annual international Composite Rules fixture is held on a home-and-away basis between Ireland and Scotland. While there are compromises in the rules, each side is permitted to use its own stick. Ireland are represented by hurlers from the second-tier Christy Ring Cup but have played second fiddle to their Gaelic cousins in recent years, with the Scots completing a four-in-a-row success over Ireland in 2008.

– BAND OF BROTHERS . . . AND SISTERS –

The Artane Band, originally the Artane Boys' Band, is synonymous with Croke Park and has been performing at GAA events for over 100 years. The band was founded in 1872 in what was then the Artane Industrial School for orphaned and abandoned boys on the north side of Dublin. The band, known as 'the biggest little band in the world', gave its first public performance for the visiting Prince of Wales in 1874. In June 1886, the band first played at a GAA event and subsequently became a central part of pre-match pageantry in Croke Park. In 1986, former band members were brought together to celebrate the centenary of their involvement with the GAA, and out of that reunion the Artane Senior Band was formed in 1988. There are 70 members of the junior band, aged between 12 and 16, and with girls now permitted to join, the name of the band has been changed to the Artane Band. On match days, 45 members, musicians and flag-bearers travel to perform. The most famous musician to emerge from the band's ranks over the years is U2 drummer Larry Mullen. The band appeared in a video for the U2 song 'The Sweetest Thing'.

– CURROW'S INTERNATIONAL GAELS –

The small mid-Kerry village of Currow near Castleisland gave rise to three promising young Gaelic footballers, all of whom, remarkably, went on to become famous international rugby players, representing Ireland and the British and Irish Lions. The late Mick Doyle, Moss Keane and Mick Galwey were all from Currow and all began their sporting careers on GAA fields.

Doyle was brought up playing Gaelic football, but left Castleisland to sit his Leaving Cert at Newbridge College in Co. Kildare, where he began playing rugby. On his return he joined Castleisland Rugby Club, but also represented UCD, Cambridge and Edinburgh universities, and played with Blackrock. Doyle won 20 caps with Ireland, played with the Lions in 1968 and famously coached Ireland to Triple Crown and Five Nations glory in 1985. Mick's younger brother Tom was a colleague of his on the Ireland rugby team and also played at midfield for the Kerry minor GAA team that won the All-Ireland of 1963.

Moss Keane won three Sigerson Cup Gaelic football medals with UCC in 1969, 1970 and 1972, and played at full-back with the Kerry juniors. He only began playing rugby seriously while at college, though he went on to make 51 appearances for Ireland between 1974 and '84, and played with the Lions in 1977. Keane was also part of the famous Munster side that defeated the All Blacks in 1977.

Mick Galwey won an All-Ireland senior medal with Kerry in 1986 as a 19 year old, as well as county championship medals at minor, junior and senior levels. He became a key figure in the All-Ireland league success of Shannon rugby club in the 1990s and was an inspirational captain with Munster. He was capped 41 times for Ireland and played with the Lions in 1993.

Kerry's connection with Irish rugby doesn't end there, of course. Dublin-born Conor O'Shea won 35 international caps with Ireland in the 1990s. Conor is a son of Jerome O'Shea – winner of the All-Ireland with Kerry in the '50s and '60s – while both Dick and Donal Spring are former International rugby players, Kingdom seniors and sons of Dan Spring, who captained Kerry to win the All-Ireland title of 1940.

– WHAT THEY SAID ABOUT THE BAN –

'I call on the young men of Ireland not to identify themselves with rugby or Association football or any other form of imported sport.'
— *T.F. O'Sullivan (1901)*

'I would like every Irishman to play the game that most appeals to him and I have no sympathy with the policy of exclusion pursued by the Gaelic Athletic Association.'
— *Seán McEntee (1931)*

'The GAA should not even entertain a motion relating to foreign games until the National flag flies over the 32 counties of a free and undivided Ireland.'
— *Motion to Congress from Tyrone (1947)*

'In many places – and they are not all in Dublin – the rule is more honoured in the breach than the observance. As matters stand, the rule is a mockery rather than a corner-stone of the Association . . . All over the country, the three rules were openly flouted.'
— *John D. Hickey (1962)*

'It is that sense of allegiance to something permanent and enduring that has always been our strength. Our rules derive not only from a desire to organise health-giving exercise but a determination to defend national values, traditions and aims. That is what has given an enduring vitality to the work of the Gaelic Athletic Association. This is the force which has forged the links that bind our members. At all times we shall continue to guard our pastimes that have enriched the national life.'
— *Dan O'Rourke (1962)*

'To remove the ban would amount to the assassination of the GAA's intrepid vitality. Ireland can ill afford to lose so valuable a prize.'
— *Breandán Mac Lua (1967)*

'The motion [to remove the ban] is not a proposal to rescind a rule but rather a proposition to alter the fundamental structure of the Association and to open the ranks to those who never accepted us for what we are.'
— *Pat Fanning (1970)*

'Let there be sounding of trumpets as the rule disappears. Nor should there be any talk of defeat. If victory there be, let it be a victory for the Association.'

– Pat Fanning (1971)

– TANGERINE DREAM –

One of the most distinctive county jerseys in Gaelic Games is the striking orange of Armagh. When their footballers reached the 1977 All-Ireland final against Dublin, the old Canal End terrace of Croke Park was awash with a sea of orange flags, a sight never quite seen before despite the popularity of flags and colours on the opposite terrace from Hill 16. However, it wasn't always that way for Armagh. Up until 1926, they wore black-and-amber jerseys similar to Kilkenny and, of course, their all-conquering club champions Crossmaglen. In 1926, Armagh reached an All-Ireland junior football final against Dublin, and to mark the occasion a special set of jerseys was knitted for the team by nuns in Omeath using orange wool. Armagh went on to win the junior All-Ireland and they've worn orange jerseys ever since. That was the first All-Ireland at any grade to go to an Ulster county.

– NAMING RIGHTS –

The people who lent their names to county GAA grounds:

Croke Park, Dublin: Name given to the sports grounds at Jones's Road in 1913 in honour of nationalist Archbishop Thomas Croke (1824–1902), one of the first patrons of the GAA.

O'Connor Park, Tullamore, Co. Offaly: Named after the ancient midlands clan of O'Connor.

Parnell Park, Dublin: Named after nineteenth-century nationalist figure and early GAA patron Charles Stewart Parnell (1846–91).

Páirc Tailteann, Navan, Co. Meath: The Tailteann Games were an ancient sporting event held in Meath in honour of Queen Tailtiu. The GAA resurrected the games as a sports festival in Croke Park in 1924.

O'Moore Park, Portlaoise, Co. Laois: Named after the ancient midlands clan of O'Moore or Ó Mórdha.

Dr Cullen Park, Carlow: Named after Rev. Bishop Dr Matthew Cullen (1864–1936), an enthusiastic supporter of the GAA.

Nowlan Park, Kilkenny: Named after a Kilkenny native, former GAA president and Sinn Féin activist James Nowlan (1855–1924).

St Conleth's Park, Newbridge, Co. Kildare: Named after St Conleth (450–519), the first Bishop of Kildare.

Pearse Park, Longford and Pearse Stadium, Galway: Named after the most famous 1916 revolutionary leader, Republican and GAA administrator Pádraig Pearse (1879–1916).

O'Rahilly Grounds, Drogheda Park, Co. Louth: Named after nationalist Michael O'Rahilly (1875–1916), who died during the Easter Rising.

Semple Stadium, Thurles, Co. Tipperary: Named in 1971 after Thurles Blues legend Tom Semple (1879–1943) who won All-Irelands with Tipp in 1900, 1906 and 1908.

Páirc Uí Chaoimh, Cork: Named after Cork native and the man considered to be the architect of modern GAA, Pádraig Ó Caoimh (1897–1964), general secretary of the GAA from 1920 to 1964.

Páirc Uí Rinn, Cork: Named after Cork hurling legend Christy Ring (1920–79). Formerly soccer stadium Flower Lodge.

Fitzgerald Stadium, Killarney, Co. Kerry: Named after Kerry football legend Dick Fitzgerald (1884–1930), who won five All-Irelands with Kerry early in the twentieth century and was the author of the first book written about Gaelic football.

Austin Stack Park, Tralee, Co. Kerry: Named after famous Irish revolutionary leader Austin Stack (1879–1929), who captained Kerry footballers to All-Ireland success in 1904.

Cusack Park, Ennis, Co. Clare and Cusack Park, Mullingar, Co. Westmeath: Named after Michael Cusack (1847–1906), founding father of the GAA and native of Carron, Co. Clare.

Fraher Field, Dungarvan, Co. Waterford: Named after Republican, administrator and referee Dan Fraher (1852–1929), who purchased the ground.

Walsh Park, Waterford: Named after local GAA figure Willie Walsh, who spearheaded the purchase of the site in the early 1920s.

McDermott Park, Carrick-on-Shannon, Co. Leitrim: Named after Seán McDermott (1883–1916), one of the leaders of the Easter Rising.

Dr Hyde Park, Roscommon: Named after Roscommon native Dr Douglas Hyde (1860–1949), first president of Ireland and famous Gaelic scholar.

Markiewicz Park, Sligo: Named after Sligo native Countess Markiewicz (1868–1927), Irish revolutionary and first woman elected to the British Parliament.

McHale Park, Castlebar, Co. Mayo: Named after John McHale (1791–1881), Archbishop of Tuam from 1831 to 1881 and celebrated Irish nationalist.

St Tiernach's Park, Clones, Co. Monaghan: Named after the founder of the sixth-century monastery in Clones.

Casement Park, Belfast, Co. Antrim: Named after Irish revolutionary Roger Casement (1864–1916).

Breffni Park, Cavan: Named after the historical kingdom of Bréifne, which included Cavan.

Brewster Park, Enniskillen, Co. Fermanagh: Named after Fermanagh footballer Mick Brewster (1937–79), who died at 42 and was the father of Fermanagh stars Paul and Tom.

MacCumhail Park, Ballybofey, Co. Donegal: Named after Seán MacCumhaill, a former chief of staff of the IRA, who died in 1949.

EXCEPTIONS PROVE THE RULE

While there exists a rule in the GAA that grounds not be named to honour people still alive, there are notable exceptions. The playing field in Cratloe, Co. Clare, is named Páirc Mhichíl Uí h-Eithir in honour of the legendary commentator Michael O'Hehir and was officially opened by the late Brendan Vaughan, then chairman of the Clare County Board, in the presence of Michael himself in July 1991.

Strange as it may seem, there is a second pitch of the same name in Clare, in Cluain Dá Ghaid, and this was officially opened by Michael O'Hehir himself in July 1993. It was close to Paradise, where his father, Jim, was born. Jim was trainer of the Clare hurling team that won the All-Ireland of 1914. He also trained the Leitrim football team of 1927 for the All-Ireland semi-final against Kerry.

– HURLING IN ARGENTINA –

Of all the global outposts in which the GAA has made an impact, Argentina's connection with hurling is one of the most striking. Ireland's links with Argentina were forged in the nineteenth century, when many immigrants travelled to South America to work on the ranches. In 1900, the Argentine Hurling Club was formed under the patronage of newspaperman William Bulfin. Bulfin published details of the game in the *Southern Cross* newspaper, and teams were formed among the Irish community with the help of priests. Hurleys were shipped from Ireland and fixtures were held regularly up until the outbreak of the First World War, when it became impossible to obtain Irish ash. Efforts were made to make hurleys using local wood, but it proved unsuitable. The game was revived for a period after 1918, but the Second World War ended the game as a popular pastime. Immigration to Argentina from Ireland petered out after 1945 and the subsequent generations of Irish-Argentines were assimilated quickly into the Argentine way of life. Hurling was played occasionally in the 1960s, but while the Argentine Hurling Club still exists today, it is now used for soccer, rugby and hockey.

– ON THE WRONG SIDE –

While Kerry's standing in Gaelic football terms is unrivalled, they have endured their share of pain on All-Ireland final day. In fact, Kerry have lost 18 finals to date, more than any other county. Down, one of the few counties to enjoy total dominance over Kerry in All-Ireland finals (they also defeated them in semi-finals in 1961 and 1991), have never lost an All-Ireland final and have five titles in the bag. Limerick and Donegal have never been defeated in football finals either, though Limerick's two crowns were won in the late nineteenth century, while Donegal have never repeated their heroics of 1992. Of the counties who have reached All-Ireland football finals, six – Laois, Monaghan, Antrim, London, Waterford, Clare – have never won. Wicklow and Fermanagh are the only two remaining counties never to have won a senior provincial football title. The Kerry hurlers are unique in that they're the only All-Ireland winners never to lose an All-Ireland final. They won the 1891 hurling All-Ireland.

– YES WE CAN –

Perhaps the proudest days of the year for any GAA president are the first and third Sundays in the month of September, when they hand the Liam MacCarthy and Sam Maguire Cups over to victorious captains of the All-Ireland Senior Hurling and Football Championships. Still, it's probably a little sweeter if they get to pass either cup to one of their 'own' in the process. Outgoing president and proud Kilkenny man Nickey Brennan had the distinction of presiding over three All-Ireland hurling wins for the Cats between 2006 and 2008, joining Cork man Con Murphy (1976, '77 and '78) as the only presidents to stand beside their own countymen as they raised the Liam MacCarthy Cup in each year in office. Paddy Buggy, who held the position between 1982 and 1985, started off well, with Kilkenny winning in the first two years of his term, before Cork scuppered a hat-trick by winning back the hurling title in 1984. For the record, only one GAA president has watched his own county win three All-Ireland football titles from just behind the podium in the Hogan Stand: Dublin's Daniel McCarthy, who served during the Dubs' three-in-a-row years of 1921, '22 and '23.

– PAYING THE PENALTY –

Penalty kicks in Gaelic football can be something of a double-edged sword, particularly in comparison to soccer. Kicking a heavier ball from further out (13 m) into a smaller goal means the scoring ratio is less than that of penalty kicks in soccer. When the shot is saved or missed, it frequently gives the opposition a lift. The penalty was first introduced to football in 1940, along with the semi-penalty in hurling, where the goalkeeper is joined on the line by two outfield players. However, missed penalties are probably remembered more vividly than those scored, including the very first penalty awarded in the football championship, which was missed by Meath in the 1940 Leinster football final against Laois, although the Royals still managed to win.

The fate of the Six Counties' bids for the Sam Maguire Cup has also been influenced by the vicissitudes of penalty taking. In the 1953 All-Ireland final, Kerry defeated Armagh by four points, but only after the Orchard County's wing-forward Bill McCorry had missed a penalty. However, the Sam eventually crossed the border in 1960 after Down defeated Kerry in the final, assisted by Paddy Doherty's goal from a penalty. The large square (parallelogram) was extended in 1970, which meant more penalties were awarded, but the misses didn't stop. In the 1974 final, Dublin keeper Paddy Cullen famously sent the Blues on the way to their first All-Ireland in 11 years when he acrobatically saved a shot from Galway's Liam Sammon.

In 1986, Tyrone, making their first All-Ireland final appearance, had the mighty Kerry team on the rack when Kevin McCabe's penalty sailed over the bar, giving them an eight-point lead instead of nine. Kerry's eventual comeback and victory left Tyrone ruing the missed opportunity, although Jack O'Shea also missed a penalty for Kerry the same day. Dublin have had a number of high-profile misses over the past couple of decades. Keith Barr missed one in the final game of the epic clash with Meath in 1991, while Charlie Redmond missed kicks in the '92 and '94 All-Ireland finals. Paul Bealin also clattered a penalty off the crossbar, the last kick of the Leinster Senior Football Championship clash with Meath in 1997, when Dublin trailed by three points. Of course, the only way to make up for a penalty miss is to go on and score the vital goal anyway, which is what Armagh's Oisín McConville did in 2002.

– SAY AGAIN? –

Four of the more unusual GAA club names:

MULLAHORAN DREADNOUGHTS: Based in Cavan, the club takes its name from the type of twentieth-century battleship first launched by the British Army in 1906. It was the first of its kind to use a steam-turbine propeller and a revolutionary type of armour that took naval battle to a new level.

LONGFORD SLASHERS: The name 'Slasher' in Irish folklore refers to Myles 'The Slasher' O'Reilly, who was, according to legend, a defender of the bridge in Finea, Co. Cavan. Slasher's mythical status was secured when he reportedly staved off over 1,000 of Cromwell's soldiers backed with just 100 men of his own.

RAPPAREES-STARLIGHTS: The Enniscorthy club is named after the Irish guerrilla warfare fighters who sided with the Jacobites during the Williamite War in 1688. Many of the Rapparees embarked upon a life of crime upon the conclusion of the war, and the term was subsequently applied to the bandits of the time.

THE FIGHTING COCKS: The Carlow club located near Rathoe takes its name, quite literally, from one of the main activities of interest down through the years. Cock fighting, now illegal, was big in the area and attracted many locals for the purposes of entertainment. and wagering on the outcome of fights between birds bred for the 'sport'. 'Fighting Cocks' itself is a small crossroads in Carlow, while the famous pub of the same name is adorned with stuffed mounts of the fallen fowl warriors.

– IMPACT-SUBS –

In 2001, Dublin football manager Tom Carr called one of the county's cult heroes, Vinny Murphy, out of intercounty retirement back into the sky-blue fold. The barrel-chested Murphy had been on an intercounty hiatus down in Kerry since falling away from the Dublin team after their All-Ireland win in 1995. Carr wasn't inclined to start Murphy in his team, though. Instead, he saw him as a substitute designed to bring maximum effect late on in games. The phrase 'impact-sub' was coined. Murphy pulled Dublin out of the fire with a brilliant late point against Offaly in the Leinster semi-final, and then against Kerry in Thurles in an All-Ireland quarter-final, he scored a goal to help Dublin claw back a seven-point lead and force a replay. Indeed, the Dubs might have won only for Kerry's very own impact-sub, Maurice Fitzgerald, who bent a stunning sideline ball over the bar from 45 m out to level the game at the death.

In 2005, though, Tyrone manager Mickey Harte brought the idea to a new level. The Red Hands' long-time source of inspiration, Peter Canavan, was hampered in the build-up to the final with an ankle injury. Harte started 'Peter the Great' and he scored the game's opening goal, but Tyrone fans were dismayed when Canavan failed to appear for the second half. However, he limbered up to the sideline in the fifty-fifth minute, re-entered the match and his second coming gave Tyrone the lift they needed to win their second All-Ireland title.

And Harte was at it again three years later. Stephen O'Neill, Footballer of the Year in 2005, having spent the year away from the Tyrone colours, was drafted back into the squad for the final against Kerry and entered the fray in the first half before setting up a goal in the second.

Of course, the most famous impact-sub of all time was Seamus Darby back in 1982 when his dramatic last-minute goal denied

Kerry the five-in-a-row. The goal was the zenith of Darby's career and one of the most memorable moments in GAA history. Seamus was also a member of Offaly's All-Ireland-winning team of 1972.

– NAME ON THE CUP –

SAM MAGUIRE CUP: 'Sam', as it is affectionately known, was first awarded to the winners of the Senior Football Championship in 1928 (Kildare). The trophy, which is modelled on the eighth-century Ardagh Chalice, is named after Cork man Sam Maguire, an IRB member who became an influential figure in the GAA in London and who had died earlier in 1928. Pat McCartan, a Tyrone man, chaired the committee to raise funds for a commemorative trophy in honour of Maguire and, after purchasing the trophy for the princely sum of £300, presented it to the GAA. The Central Council then decreed that the new trophy would be presented to the All-Ireland senior football champions from then on, and it was first awarded to Kildare's Bill 'Squires' Gannon. Incidentally, the cup that is presented to winning captains now is a replacement. The original was shelved following the 1987 championship due to the wear and tear Sam had suffered over the previous 60 years. Sam Maguire played for London in the All-Ireland finals of 1900, 1901 and 1903.

TOMMY MURPHY CUP: In 2004, the GAA introduced a secondary football championship for counties eliminated from both provincial competitions and the early stages of the All-Ireland qualifiers, naming the cup after the prominent Laois footballer Tommy Murphy, who was one of the midfielders selected on the GAA's Team of the Millennium. However, due to a low level of interest in the competition, it was scrapped following the 2008 season.

LIAM MACCARTHY CUP: Presented for the All-Ireland senior hurling championship, the cup actually outdates the big-ball equivalent, having been first awarded to the winning captain of the All-Ireland Hurling Championship in 1921, Bob McConkey (Limerick). Liam MacCarthy was a former chairman of the London County Board, vice president of the Gaelic League and president of the Irish Athletic Association, and had the trophy made in the design of an ancient Gaelic Meither. After donating the cup to the GAA, the Central Council elected to honour MacCarthy himself by naming the trophy after him and awarding the cup to the All-Ireland senior hurling champions.

CHRISTY RING CUP: The trophy for the second-tier hurling championship was named after arguably the greatest hurler of all time, Christy Ring. Ring won eight All-Ireland titles with Cork in an intercounty career that spanned twenty-five years, scoring 33–208 in sixty-four championship outings. The competition itself came into being in 2005, with Westmeath beating Down in that year's final in Croke Park.

NICKY RACKARD CUP: Commissioned in 2005 as a prize for the winners of the Division 3 Championship. Nicky Rackard was a Wexford forward of undeniable talent, claiming two All-Irelands with the county (1955 and '56), and he remains Wexford's all-time highest scorer in championship hurling, with a tally of 29–96 in thirty-six games. London were the inaugural winners of the cup, with the champions now qualifying for a spot in the Christy Ring Cup.

LORY MEAGHER CUP: In 2008, the GAA decided to rejig their hurling championship structures and added a fourth layer to the competitions. The new cup was named after Lory Meagher, the double All-Ireland-winning Kilkenny midfielder of the same name. Meagher, Rackard and Ring were all named on the GAA's hurling Team of the Century back in 1984, while Meagher and Ring were also both honoured with places on the GAA's hurling Team of the Millennium in 2000.

– CAPITAL SPLIT –

In 2002, a strategic review carried out by the GAA under the chairmanship of former Association president Peter Quinn proposed that Dublin, with its disproportionate population, should be split into two separate football divisions. The proposal envisaged that the city would be divided by the Liffey into two separate football 'counties' – North and South – with separate county boards. However, hurlers were to continue to compete as a single county unit. While there was a positive response to the suggestion from outside the capital, Dublin supporters were up in arms, with petitions quickly circulated by fans to oppose any attempts to introduce partition. The proposal was never implemented.

– FREAK INJURY –

One often hears the term 'freak injury' used to describe some knock or other picked up by a sportsperson outside matches or the confines of the training ground. A freak injury sometimes involves a player falling down stairs, straining his arm reaching for the remote control, or slipping in the shower, but for unfortunate Donegal footballer Paddy McConigley, his intercounty career-ending injury really *was* a complete freak. In 2007, McConigley, along with his Donegal teammates, were taken on a team-bonding exercise to a paintballing course, and in one of the games, a paint pellet fired at high velocity managed to evade McConigley's goggles and hit him in his left eye. He underwent surgery to save the sight in the eye, but emerged with just 5 per cent vision. His intercounty career was sadly ended at the tender age of just 26.

I once witnessed a freak accident in the Meath dressing-room prior to one of their 1991 four-game-saga matches with Dublin. While lifting his leg to remove his jeans, Terry Ferguson's back went into spasm, and despite the presence of team manager and herbalist Seán Boylan, and teammate and doctor Gerry McEntee, he failed to recover and had to be replaced prior to the start of the game.

– NINE OUT OF TEN CATS PREFER –

The golden era of Brian Cody's Kilkenny hurling team's three-in-a-row years of 2006 to 2008 also coincided with the re-emergence to competitive league action of the county's footballers. It's probably unfair to the big-ballers within the county to be comparing them to their awesome hurling countymen, but the contrast between their fortunes couldn't have been any starker. True, Kilkenny haven't won a senior football championship match since they beat Louth in 1929 and they famously had to field a young mascot to make up their numbers in 1914, but they have had one notable success since reinstatement to the National League. On 13 April 2008, the Cats met London in Nowlan Park, with only the avoidance of the bottom-tier wooden spoon to play for. And in a tense finale, they beat the Exiles by 2–13 to 0–15. That, unfortunately, was to prove the high-water mark of their football fortunes for a while, and the following season they suffered heavy defeat after heavy defeat in successive weeks.

The April 2008 experience was my strangest yet at a sporting event, for on the same day I saw the Kilkenny hurlers lose and the footballers win.

In 2009, London gained revenge for their reversal with an emphatic 2–12 to 0–7 in Ruislip. In fact, Kilkenny failed to score a single goal until their final-day defeat to Carlow. Over the course of their eight 2009 NFL games, Kilkenny averaged just 5.25 points per game and conceded a whopping 31.75.

KILKENNY'S 2009 NFL DIVISION 4 RESULTS

Kilkenny 0–4 Sligo 3–20

Kilkenny 0–5 Antrim 4–27

Kilkenny 0–3 Waterford 2–20

Kilkenny 0–3 Wicklow 7–24

Kilkenny 0–4 Clare 5–23

Kilkenny 0–4 Leitrim 4–19

Kilkenny 0–7 London 2–12

Kilkenny 1–9 Carlow 2–22

Played: 8 Won: 0 Draw: 0 Lost: 8

For: 1–39 Against: 29–167 Diff.: -212 Pts: 0

– PASSING THE SCREEN TEST –

The 1962 All-Ireland hurling final was a seminal moment in the history of Irish broadcasting and the GAA as it was the first All-Ireland final televised live on Ireland's new Teilifís Éireann. The first radio broadcast of a game had taken place 36 years earlier, on 29 August 1926, when commentary on the All-Ireland hurling semi-final between Kilkenny and Galway crackled into the homes of Irish people. It was the first radio commentary on a field sport outside of America, and radio coverage of Gaelic Games, in particular the voice of legendary commentator Michael O'Hehir, played a vital role in the growth of the GAA during the twentieth century. And the bilingual commentary was shared by Seán Óg Ó Ceallacháin and I.

The televised decider in 1962, however, was a new departure. The game was an eagerly awaited clash between Tipperary, bidding to retain their crown after beating Dublin the previous year, and Wexford, who had defeated the Premier County in the 1960 final. Despite conceding two early goals, Wexford battled back, and the game was in the balance until the late stages, when points from Tipp's Donie Nealon and Seán McLoughlin secured the victory.

The high-scoring 1971 All-Ireland hurling final between Tipp and Kilkenny became the first game to be televised in colour, and viewers were served a feast as Tipperary defeated the Cats 5–17 to 5–14. Up until 1989, the only games RTÉ was permitted to show live were the All-Ireland semi-finals and finals. However, in '89 the restrictions were relaxed, and RTÉ showed the Munster hurling final between Tipperary and Waterford live. Today, the rights for competitive intercounty games are sold by the GAA to a number of television stations, although RTÉ possesses the rights to the vast majority of key fixtures, showing over 50 championship games live per season. In 2008, 46 years after Tipp and Wexford first appeared in black and white, over 840,000 people tuned in to RTÉ to watch Kilkenny defeat Waterford in the All-Ireland hurling final.

– FOOD OF CHAMPIONS –

Dieticians are a permanent feature on most of today's county management teams, with regular nutritional advice considered vital for the ambitious hurler and footballer. However, the latest trend jars with the experience of former Kerry midfielder Pat McCarthy. The morning of the 1975 All-Ireland final clash with Dublin, a light snack was prepared for the Kerry team before they were due to set off to Croke Park. At the same time, the accompanying party of county board officials was planning to sit down to a full four-course lunch. McCarthy arrived in the dining room unaware of the designated scale of the repast and proceeded to polish off the four courses intended for the officials – including roast beef, potatoes and apple pie – just two hours before an All-Ireland final. With a full stomach, McCarthy played a stormer at midfield as Kerry's team of bachelors upset the reigning champions. Food for thought.

– THE GREATEST GOAL EVER? –

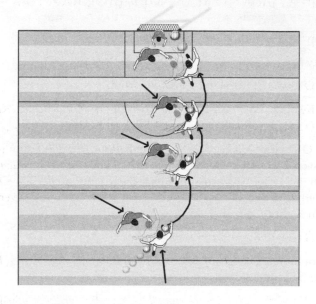

While debate will never cease as to the greatest goal in Gaelic football, for sheer technical ability and quick-fire skill, Eoin Mulligan's goal versus Dublin in Croke Park on 13 August 2005 is hard to rival. I once met Eoin's mother, who told me she never opened her mouth during matches for fear she would do something wrong. But she said that when he scored that goal, she let out a roar: 'That's my son!' She simply couldn't contain herself.

– PRESIDENTIAL SNUB –

Douglas Hyde, the first president of Ireland, was also the first man to have his patronage of the GAA withdrawn. The conflict between the statesman and the Association came after Hyde, a close confidant of Michael Cusack during the formation of the GAA, attended an international soccer match in his capacity as president. However, this didn't sit too well with the newly formed Gaelic Athletic Association, of whom Hyde was a patron, and so they suspended the founder of the Gaelic League.

– PRINT THAT:
PLAYER AND MANAGER BIOGRAPHIES –

Tommy Doyle: *A Lifetime in Hurling* (1955).

Christy Ring: *Christy Ring* (1980) by Val Dorgan.

Mick O'Connell: *A Kerry Footballer* (1974).

Babs Keating: *Babs, a Legend in Irish Sport: The Michael Keating Story* (1996) by Donal Keenan and Michael Keating.

Mick O'Dwyer: *Mick O'Dwyer: The Authorised Biography* (1990) by Owen McCrohan; *Mick O'Dwyer: Manager of the Millennium* (2000) by Owen McCrohan; *Blessed and Obsessed: The Official Autobiography of Mick O'Dwyer* (2007) by Mick O'Dwyer with Martin Breheny.

Liam Hayes: *Out of Our Skins* (1992).

Dermot Earley: *The Earley Years: Official Biography of Dermot Earley* (1992) by John Scally.

Nicky English: *Beyond the Tunnel* (1996) by Nicky English with Vincent Hogan.

Terence McNaughton: *'Sambo': All or Nothing* (1998).

Pat Spillane: *Shooting from the Hip: The Pat Spillane Story* (1998) by Pat Spillane and Sean McGoldrick.

John O'Leary: *Back to the Hill: The Official Biography* (1997).

Ger Loughnane: *Raising the Banner: Official Biography of Ger Loughnane* (2001) by John Scally.

Páidí Ó Sé: *Páidí: The Life of Gaelic Football Legend Páidí Ó Sé* (2001) by Páidí Ó Sé and Seán Potts.

Liam Dunne: *I Crossed the Line* (2004) by Liam Dunne and Damian Lawlor.

Dessie Farrell: *Dessie: Tangled Up in Blue* (2005) by Dessie Farrell and Seán Potts.

Davy Fitzgerald: *Passion and Pride: The Official Biography of Davy Fitzgerald* (2005) by Jackie Cahill.

Charlie Carter: *Triumph and Troubles: The Official Biography of Charlie Carter* (2005) by Enda McAvoy.

Graham Geraghty: *Misunderstood* (2006) by Graham Geraghty and J. Doyle.

Brian Corcoran: *Every Single Ball: The Brian Corcoran Story* (2006) by Brian Corcoran and Kieran Shannon.

Seán Boylan: *Seán Boylan: The Will to Win* (2006) by Seán Boylan and John Quinn.

Oisín McConville: *The Gambler: Oisín McConville's Story* (2007) by Oisín McConville and Ewan MacKenna.

Jack O'Connor: *Keys to the Kingdom* (2007) by Tom Humphries.

Seán Óg de Paor: *Lá an Phaoraigh* (2008) by Seán Óg de Paor and Aoife de Paor.

Dan O'Neill: *Divided Loyalties: The Life and Times of a Mayo Man Who Won an All-Ireland Title with Louth in 1957* (2008).

– 'CHICKS WITH STICKS': CAMOGIE TIMELINE –

Camogie is the women's form of hurling and is almost identical to the men's game except for a number of rule differences, such as using a smaller sliotar and the shoulder charge not being permitted. The Camogie Association was formed for women in 1904, and the game has developed very successfully alongside hurling. Camogie is now a hugely popular participation sport in Ireland with over 100,000 playing the game. After the centenary of the Camogie Association in 2004, it was decided to adopt a sexy new slogan to promote the game, and the phrase 'chicks with sticks' was born, with a picture of players in evening dress carrying hurleys used in one sports magazine.

1904: Women's variant of hurling is launched officially with the first public match played in Meath between Craobh a'Chéitinigh and Cúchulainn's.

1905: Máire Ní Chinnéide becomes the first president of the Camogie Association.

1912: First county camogie match played at the sports grounds on Jones's Road.

1915: Ashbourne Cup, the oldest competition in camogie, is established for third-level colleges.

1932: Dublin win the inaugural All-Ireland Senior Camogie Championship.

1934: Provincial councils of the Camogie Association are set up.

1936: Cork complete camogie's first senior three-in-a-row of All-Irelands.

1954: First interpros take place, with the competition set up on an annual basis two years later.

1955: Dublin win their eighth senior All-Ireland title in a row.

1964: New All-Ireland Camogie Club Championships mark the 60th anniversary of the Association.

1974: Minor and Junior Colleges Championships set up. Camogie included in Féile na nGael.

1979: Junior National League inaugurated. New tournament for the Gaeltacht clubs.

1980: First full-time director appointed to Camogie Association. Office set up at GAA headquarters in Croke Park.

1992: First All-Ireland Intermediate Championship won by the Dubs.

1995: Foras na Gaeilge become Camogie's first title sponsor.

1999: Fifteen-a-side teams and full hurling pitch introduced.

2000: Laois win first All-Ireland Minor B Championship.

2003: Crossmaglen win first All-Ireland Junior Club Championship.

2004: Centenary anniversary celebrated with announcement of Team of the Century. First All-Star Camogie team announced. Organisation reported to have close to 100,000 members. First Camogie Poc Fada takes place on Cooley Mountains. 'Chicks with sticks' promotional slogan adopted for the sport.

2006: Camogie grows in popularity to unprecedented levels, with over 515 clubs in operation.

– GER LOUGHNANE: BEST VALUE –

It has been said of controversial former Clare hurling legend Ger Loughnane that 'nobody gives better quotes or better value'. Hard to disagree.

'We've got grounds which are state of the art and administration which is state of the ark.'

> *– Ger Loughnane on one of his*
> *myriad clashes with GAA officials*

'I don't think Henry Kissinger would have lasted a week on the Munster Council.'

> *– Ditto*

'I'm not giving away any secrets like that to Tipperary. If I had my way, I wouldn't even tell them the time of the throw-in.'

> *– Ger Loughnane reacting to criticisms of his*
> *misleading Clare team announcements in the press*

'Ger Loughnane was fair; he treated us all the same during training: like dogs.'

> *– Anonymous Clare hurler on*
> *Loughnane's infamous training regime*

'The first thing I would do is purchase a gun and leave it to my wife at home. Because if I ever insinuate that I'm returning to county management, then I'll tell her to have me shot straight away. It's something you should do once, and once only.'

> *– Ger Loughnane on retiring as*
> *Clare hurling manager in 2000*

'I've been six years a pundit. Life goes in phases. I had a phase as a player, then I had a phase as a manager of my own county. I went into analysis for a few years and now I'm back into management. It is time.'

> *– Ger Loughnane on returning to*
> *management with Galway in 2006*

'I was on the Hurling Development Committee, which tried to persuade Galway to come into the Leinster Championship. When we met them, *one official* fell asleep at the end of the table. That's a fact. *Another official*'s only concern was that the kitchen was closing at 9 p.m., so the meeting had to be over before then, so that he'd get his meal. They weren't the slightest bit interested.'

– Ger Loughnane letting rip at Galway
officials after he ceased to be manager in October 2008

'The funny thing is, I have no luck with priests! It was a priest from Killenana, a "Fr McNamara", who is now in a club in Galway, who had promised to vote for us, and then 20 minutes before the vote started, he told John Fahy that he had to vote against us, because the chairman had rung him up. So we were tripped up by a priest again.'

– Ditto

'Ballinasloe is like a sheep field. Loughrea is an absolute disgrace – a tiny, cabbage garden of a field. Athenry is the worst of all. I asked myself: what were these people doing in the 1980s when they had all this success? It was Pearse Stadium they concentrated on – the stand, not the pitch. Because the pitch is like something left over from Famine times, there are so many ridges in it. It has left Galway bereft of any decent hurling facility. But you get over that!'

– Ger Loughnane on Galway's hurling facilities

'Not only is there "history" between every two clubs in Galway, there is history between every two people in Galway that I meet.'

– Ger Loughnane on Galway

– LIST OF 'FOREIGN' GAMES PLAYED IN CROKE PARK –

SOCCER

Irish Cup
1901: Cliftonville v Freebooters*

Euro 2008 Qualifiers
24 March 2007: Republic of Ireland v Wales
28 March 2007: Republic of Ireland v Slovakia
13 October 2007: Republic of Ireland v Germany
17 October 2007: Republic of Ireland v Cyprus

Friendlies
6 February 2008: Republic of Ireland v Brazil
24 May 2008: Republic of Ireland v Serbia

World Cup 2010 Qualifiers
15 October 2008: Republic of Ireland v Cyprus
11 February 2009: Republic of Ireland v Georgia
28 March 2009: Republic of Ireland v Bulgaria
10 October 2009: Republic of Ireland v Italy
14 October 2009: Republic of Ireland v Montenegro

RUGBY UNION

RBS Six Nations 2007
11 February 2007: Ireland v France
24 February 2007: Ireland v England

RBS Six Nations 2008
2 February 2008: Ireland v Italy
23 February 2008: Ireland v Scotland
8 March 2008: Ireland v Wales

International Test Matches
15 March 2008: Ireland v New Zealand
22 November 2008: Ireland v Argentina

---

* The ground was called Jones's Road Stadium at the time and was not owned by the GAA.

RBS Six Nations 2009
7 February 2009: Ireland v France
28 February 2009: Ireland v England

Heineken Cup Semi-Final 2009
2 May 2009: Leinster v Munster

AMERICAN FOOTBALL

1946: Exhibition game between American soldiers
2 November 1996: Notre Dame v Navy
27 July 1997: Pittsburgh Steelers v Chicago Bears

BOXING

19 July 1972: Muhammad Ali v Al 'Blue' Lewis

BASEBALL

1946: Burtonwood Dodgers v Mildenhall Yankees

– CROSS-BORDER BROTHERS –

There are plenty of families with strong GAA traditions, but the Carr brothers, Tommy and Declan, have the distinction of being the only brothers to have won All-Stars in football and hurling (Tommy in football and Declan in hurling). What makes their achievement all the more remarkable is that they managed it with two different counties. Though born in Dublin, Declan went on to play hurling for Tipperary, where he lived at the time, and won All-Ireland medals in 1989 and 1991. Declan was awarded an All-Star for his performances in 1989, and the family name would bring further recognition, albeit in a different code and a different county, when Tommy began playing football for Dublin. Tommy won his All-Star in 1991, though Declan was denied the hurling gong despite captaining the Premier County to Liam MacCarthy success that same year. Later, Tommy would go on to manage Dublin, Roscommon and Cavan, while Declan presided over the Tipperary team that were beaten in the All-Ireland under-21 final by Kilkenny in 2008.

- THE LAND DOWN UNDER -

A fear has persisted in the GAA for some time that the lure of a professional career in Australian Rules could eventually lead to a substantial drain of young talent from Gaelic football. It should, however, be pointed out that very few Irishmen have ever really made it in the Australian Football League (AFL). There are currently eight former GAA players on contracts in Australia, with Martin Clarke and Setanta Ó hAilpín the only ones to feature regularly in the 2008–09 season for Collingwood and Carlton Blues, respectively.

Five players have come home since 2007, either having failed to settle in Australia or having been released by their clubs. In total, 26 Irish players have held contracts in Australia, the first of whom was Kerryman Seán Wight, who was brought over by Melbourne legend Ron Barassi in 1982 in what was dubbed the 'Irish Experiment'. Wight was an immediate success, although a knee injury eventually curtailed his career. He also excelled at rugby and cricket cross channel.

However, the Irish player who made the biggest impact in Australia was Jim Stynes. Having starred in Dublin's All-Ireland minor-title-winning team of 1984, Stynes was subsequently recruited by Barassi and travelled to Melbourne. By the end of an 11-year first-team career (1987–98), Stynes had broken the league record for consecutive AFL games with 244, achieved All-Australians in 1991 and '93, and was awarded the prestigious Brownlow Medal in 1991. Stynes was also inducted into the Australian Hall of Fame in 2003, and in 2008 he became chairman of Melbourne Demons.

The one jewel missing from Stynes's collection, though, is an AFL Premiership medal, but there is one Irish player in possession of that gong: Kerryman Tadhg Kennelly. A promising Kerry underage player, and son of the late Kerry legend Tim, Kennelly was snapped up by Sydney Swans in 1999 and made his debut in 2001, following his elevation from the rookie list. Swans, with Kennelly playing all 26 games from start to finish, won the AFL Premiership crown in 2005, and almost claimed back-to-back titles the following year, but lost by a single point to West Coast Eagles. Kennelly retired after the 2008 season and is back in Ireland playing Gaelic football with Kerry.

Irish players currently in Australia: Setanta Ó hAilpín (Cork, Carlton); Martin Clarke (Down, Collingwood); Kevin Dyas (Armagh,

Collingwood); Michael Quinn (Longford, Essendon); Brendan Murphy (Carlow, Sydney); Colm Begley (Laois, St Kilda); Pearse Hanley (Mayo, Brisbane); Conor Meredith (Laois, North Melbourne).

And those who have returned within the past two years: Tadhg Kennelly (Kerry, Sydney); Aisake Ó hAilpín (Cork, Carlton); Kyle Coney (Tyrone, Sydney); Michael Shields (Cork, Carlton); Brendan Quigley (Laois, Brisbane).

Other Irish players who have had professional contracts with AFL clubs: Jim Stynes (Dublin, Melbourne); James Fahy (Dublin, Melbourne); Brian Stynes (Dublin, Melbourne); Niall Buckley (Kildare, Melbourne); Colin Corkery (Cork, Melbourne); Bernie Collins (Cork, Western Bulldogs); Seán Wight (Kerry, Melbourne); Paul Earley (Roscommon, Melbourne); Colm McManamon (Mayo, Geelong); Nicholas Walsh (Cavan, Melbourne); Dermot McNicholl (Derry, St Kilda); Anthony Tohill (Derry, Melbourne).

– DENIS JOSEPH CAREY –

The Kilkenny hurling landscape has been shaped by some of the most skilful and successful exponents of the art, but close followers of hurling on Noreside knew they were on to something special by the time Denis Joseph Carey made his minor bow for the Cats aged 17. By then, he was known simply by his initials: D.J.

What set him apart from his peers is not so much measured in medals or statistics, though he has plenty of both. With five All-Ireland titles, ten Leinster crowns, four National Hurling League medals and nine All-Stars, D.J. can hardly be described as an underachiever. And, by bagging 34–195 in 57 championship appearances, his scores-per-game ratio ranks alongside the greatest of all time.

What Carey will be remembered for are his feats of mesmeric stickwork, brilliant improvisation and incredible vision, and as one of the deadliest finishers the game has ever known. Carey's genius prompted the frequent debate throughout his career about which hurler was better: Ring, Mackey, Keher or D.J.?

Regardless of opinion, some of the Gowran man's moments of magic will live on in GAA folklore long after they've started to compare the latest prodigy to the great D.J, Christy and the other masters.

GREAT D.J. MOMENTS

1. **All-Ireland senior hurling championship semi-final in 1993 v Antrim:** With Kilkenny cruising to an All-Ireland final victory and 3–13 to 1–9 ahead of the Ulster champions, Carey collected a ball 50 m from goal and sped past Paul McKillan. He angled a pass out to the left corner to P.J. Delaney, but kept going towards goal. Delaney rocketed a pass across the square, where Carey pulled first time at head height. The sliotar cannoned off the crossbar back to D.J., who showed incredible reflexes to bury it at the second time of asking with a reverse swing.

2. **All-Ireland hurling semi-final in 2002 v Tipperary:** Typical D.J. Judging the flight of a line ball to perfection, Carey gathered and, surrounded by three Tipp defenders, swivelled right then left, wrong-footing all three, before accelerating towards Brendan Cummins's goal and pointing over.

3. **All-Ireland final in 2002 v Clare:** John Hoyne directed the ball into Carey's path and he flicked up and shrugged off Liam Doyle in one movement. He caught again and shaped to go away from goal, but swerved infield, sending Ollie Baker to the floor. Having already handled the ball twice, Carey stopped the sliotar dead on his hurl and put it straight between the uprights for a breathtaking game-winning point.

WHAT THEY SAID ABOUT D.J.

'He brought everything to hurling. He's a great tackler, he's a great player, he's a great winner of a ball. His skills – he just had them all. And he's been the most exciting player in hurling for a long, long time.'

– Brian Cody

'Under every category of defining a great player, he is without doubt the finest player of his generation, if not ever. There's no doubt about it, he's the finest player I've ever seen.'

– Ger Loughnane

'They can come and go, but there will only ever be one D.J. Carey. You can talk about all the greats you like.'

– Cyril Farrell

– FINAL FORWARDS –

It's hardly surprising that the record to date for the highest scorer in an All-Ireland football final is still jointly held by two opponents from the great Dublin–Kerry rivalry of the 1970s. Dublin's Jimmy Keaveney broke the record in the 1977 decider when he scored 2–6 against Armagh, but he only held the record on his own for two years until Kerry rival Mikey Sheehy matched it exactly, scoring 2–6 against Dublin in the 1979 final. Kerry full-forward Eoin 'Bomber' Liston almost broke it in-between those years when he scored 3–2 against the Dubs in 1978.

However, while Keaveney, Sheehy and Bomber have secured their place in the history books, the scoring feats of Tyrone's Peter Canavan in the 1995 final and the late Frank Stockwell of Galway in the 1956 final stand out in their own right. Canavan delivered one of the most extraordinary individual displays in an All-Ireland final when he scored eleven of his side's twelve-point total against Dublin, almost single-handedly winning the game, although ten of the eleven scores came from frees. As most of the feats of high scoring over the years are attributed to free-takers, pride of place must therefore go to Stockwell, who kicked 2–5 from play in the '56 decider as Galway defeated Cork. He put the ball in the net a third time later that match, but the 'goal' was disallowed.

– HEALING THE WOUNDS OF WAR –

Gaelic football played a crucial role in healing the wounds of the Civil War in Ireland (1922–3), particularly in Kerry, where the local battles between the IRA and the Free State forces were the most brutal. A number of vicious atrocities were carried out by both sides, but remarkably, by the time the conflict subsided in 1923, Kerry reached the next All-Ireland final with players fresh from the jails and internment camps, some of whom had been mortal enemies during the Civil War, lining out together. The 1923 All-Ireland wasn't played until September 1924, when Kerry lost to Dublin, but they stopped a four-in-a-row for Dublin in April 1924 when they won the delayed 1924 title. Paradoxically, the war sowed the seeds of Kerry's subsequent dominance of Gaelic football between 1923 and '41, when the county won 11 All-Ireland titles, including a four-in-a-row between 1929 and '32.

Con Brosnan, a former IRA hero during the War of Independence and a subsequent officer in the new Free State Army, was seen as the bridge-builder in the squad and kicked the winning point in the 1924 final. He teamed up with anti-Treaty activists such as John Joe Sheehy and Joe Barrett, and their differences were set aside for the cause of Kerry football.

Staunch Republican Barrett, from the Rock Street club in Tralee, was captain of the successful Kerry teams of 1929 and '32. In Kerry, the county champions get to nominate the county captain, and as Joe's club, Rock Street (renamed Austin Stacks after the death of the patriot in 1929) had won the county championship again in 1930, they nominated Barrett to skipper the county side in 1931. However, in a gesture that resonates to this day, Barrett handed the captaincy over to Con Brosnan from Moyvane, his one-time Civil War enemy but subsequent lifelong friend. Barrett's actions caused deep resentment among Republicans in Tralee and in his own club, but he was supported by teammates John Joe 'Purty' Landers and Tim 'Roundy' Landers. Barrett was vindicated when Brosnan brought the Sam Maguire back to the Kingdom for the third year in a row, in 1931.

– LIKE FATHER LIKE SON –

An intercounty Gaelic football team of sons with accomplished footballing fathers.

FATHERS	SONS
Ogie Moran	David Moran
Jack O'Shea	Aidan O'Shea
Sean Walsh	Tommy, Barry and John Walsh
Bernard Brogan	Alan, Bernard and Paul Brogan
Jimmy Kerrigan	Paul Kerrigan
Mick Donnellan	John Donnellan
John Donnellan	Michael Donnellan
Frank McGuigan	Brian and Tommy McGuigan
Noel Curran	Paul Curran
Kevin McConnell	Kevin McConnell Jr
Kevin McConnell Jr	Ross McConnell
Liam O'Neill	Kevin O'Neill
Tim Kennelly	Tadhg and Noel Kennelly
James McCartan	James McCartan Jnr
Dermot Earley	Dermot Earley Jnr
John Joe Sheehy	Paudie, Niall and Seán Óg Sheehy
Joe Barrett	J.J. Barrett
Jack Myers	Billy Myers
Pat Reynolds	Paddy Reynolds
Des 'Snitchie' Ferguson	Terry Ferguson
Jap Finlay	Paul Finlay

– MINOR CELEBRITIES –

Tyrone minor footballers have enjoyed spectacular success in recent years, claiming All-Ireland titles in 1998, 2002, 2004 and 2008. In all, the county has won the Tom Markham Cup seven times, the fourth most successful county at this grade behind Kerry, Dublin and Cork. One of those successes came in 1948 when the team featured Barney Eastwood at wing-forward as Tyrone defeated Dublin by 0–11 to 1–5. Eastwood, of course, went on to become one of boxing's top promoters, managing Dave 'Boy' MacAuley and, most famously, Barry McGuigan.

Another Tyrone minor to make his name outside of Gaelic Games was snooker star Dennis Taylor, from Coalisland. Taylor played with the Red Hand minors in the 1960s, but went on to cement his international reputation by winning the 1985 World Snooker Championship in dramatic circumstances, beating Steve Davis on the black ball.

– EVEN THE GREATEST HAS TO GO –

Unlike many of Muhammad Ali's comeback bouts, his meeting with Al 'Blue' Lewis in Croke Park on 19 July 1972 was widely regarded by boxing aficionados as a good, high-quality fight. Those who thought 'The Greatest' looked comfortable throughout were a little shy of the mark, though.

Following the tenth round, Ali told his trainer, Angelo Dundee, that he was in urgent need of a toilet and that he wasn't quite sure how long he could hold on for. It would have been a strange chapter in the career of boxing's most famous figure had he left the fight to relieve himself, but such was Ali's appetite for victory, he managed to finish the contest.

Promoter Harold Conrad had set up the fight, having long trumpeted the idea of staging a heavyweight boxing match in Ireland – and who better to sell the tickets than Ali? Conrad came up with the $200,000 necessary to secure Ali's signature, and once he was on board, Croke Park was the only venue in Ireland with the capacity to stage one of his fights.

Lewis, an ex-con from Detroit, would provide the opposition. The buzz in Dublin was palpable in the days and weeks leading up to the fight, with Ali memorably appearing on RTÉ television and producing a hugely charismatic performance in conversation with Cathal O'Shannon. The pair spoke for 52 minutes in front of a studio audience, and afterwards, Shannon revealed that he had had to go into the RTÉ canteen to cash a cheque for his guest after Dundee insisted his charge be paid in cash.

The fight became the talk of the town and tickets were in scarce supply. In fact, many of those without tickets barged their way into Croke Park anyway, just to get a look at the most famous sportsperson of all time.

In the days leading up to the showdown, Ali contracted flu and was advised not to fight by doctors, but he elected to go ahead with the bout anyway, promising to knock Lewis out in the fifth round. He almost fulfilled his prophecy. Having knocked his opponent down in the fifth, Ali failed to immediately retreat to his corner and the count was extended to 15 seconds, allowing Lewis the extra time to regain his bearings.

From there, it got a little uncomfortable for Ali. Eventually, Ali finished off the job, hammering Lewis early in the eleventh round, and the fight was stopped. But Ali's agony didn't quite end there. Having stopped his opponent, Ali's fans rushed to the ring and its surrounding areas, denying him the opportunity to 'go'. It took Ali 25 minutes to back out of the ring and reach the bathroom.

– SIMPLY THE OLDEST –

Anyone who has ever toiled as a junior club hurler or footballer can recount tales of coming up against a wizened old corner-back, or an 'ancient' keeper still plying his trade well into, or even beyond, middle age. Club players, particularly hurlers, are often prepared to tog out well into their 60s, men like the celebrated Tim Byrnes of the Pádraig Pearses club in Galway, who was still hurling away with his club 36 years after winning a Fitzgibbon Cup with UCG in 1970. On the county stage, Christy Ring's reputation as one of the greatest was enhanced by his endurance – he played at the top level until a hip injury ended his career in 1963, when he was 43 years of age. However, the oldest recorded player to operate at county level was Pat Leamy, who was a sprightly 54 when he lined out in goal for New York against Tipperary in the 1951 National Hurling League final.

– ONCE UPON A TIME IN FOOTBALL –

The All-Time Football All-Star Award was run in association with the All-Stars between 1980 and 1994. This is a complete list of the winners of that award.

1980: Larry Stanley: Captained Kildare footballers to All-Ireland glory in 1919 and was an Irish Olympic high jumper. He also won an All-Ireland with Dublin in 1923, and in-between he played for Belfast Celtic.

1981: Tommy Murphy: Laois football star played in the 1937 All-Ireland semi-final against Kerry as a 16 year old. Known as the 'Boy Wonder', he gave his name to the Tommy Murphy Cup. Named at midfield on GAA's Team of the Millennium.

1982: Paddy Moclair: Full-forward on the 1936 All-Ireland-winning Mayo side and winner of six National Leagues.

1983: Jim McCullagh: Rated as one of the greatest Armagh footballers of all time. Came to prominence with Ulster, winning three Railway Cup medals in 1942, '43 and '47.

1984: John Dunne: Galway star of the 1930s, won All-Irelands in 1934 and again as captain in '38. Part of the backroom team when they won in '56 and the three-in-a-row years of 1964 to '66.

1985: The Landers brothers, John Joe 'Purty' and Tim 'Roundy': John Joe was a star of the 1929 and '30 All-Ireland-winning Kerry teams, with Tim joining him to complete the four-in-a-row in '31 and '32. Both won another All-Ireland together in '37, while Tim also played on the winning teams in '39 and '41. They also had another brother, Bill 'Lang', who won All-Irelands in 1924 and '32.

1986: Alf Murray: Starred for Armagh and Ulster between 1935 and '45, president of the GAA between '64 and '67.

1987: Mick Higgins: Played the Polo Grounds final for Cavan in 1947. Added two more All-Irelands in '48 and '52 as captain.

1988: Kevin Armstrong: Antrim legend, a dual star with the county during the 1940s and '50s. He also played in the All-Ireland hurling final of 1923.

1989: Peter McDermott: Won two All-Irelands with Meath in 1949 and '54, and refereed the 1953 final in-between. Helped establish the Compromise Rules Series with Australia.

1990: Eddie Boyle: Louth and Leinster star of the 1930s and '40s. Won five Railway Cups in '35, '39, '40, '44 and '45.

1991: Sean Purcell: Galway star of the 1956 All-Ireland-winning team. Considered one of the greatest footballers of all time, he was named on the GAA's Team of the Century and Team of the Millennium. Formed a devastating partnership with Frank Stockwell.

1992: Sean Flanagan: Captained Mayo to All-Ireland glory in 1950 and '51. Named on the GAA's Team of the Century and Team of the Millennium.

1993: Jimmy Murray: Captained Roscommon to win the 1943 and '44 All-Irelands. One of a select few to lift the Sam Maguire twice as captain.

1994: Bill Delaney: Starred for Laois and Leinster in the 1930s and '40s. Won four Leinster titles and five Railway Cups. Refereed two All-Irelands and was a long-serving administrator.

– ALL-TIME HURLING ALL-STARS –

The All-Time Hurling All-Star Award was run in association with the football All-Stars from 1980 until 1994.

1980: Mick Mackey: Legendary Limerick hurler between 1930 and '47. Won three All-Irelands. Named at centre-forward on the Team of the Century and the Team of the Millennium and considered one of the greatest hurlers ever.

1981: Jack Lynch: The former Taoiseach won six consecutive All-Irelands between 1941 and '46, five hurling and one football. Midfielder on the Team of the Century and the Team of the Millennium.

1982: Garrett Howard: Won All-Irelands with Limerick in 1921, '34 and '36, and with Dublin in '24 and '27. He won Railway Cup medals with both Leinster and Munster.

1983: Pat 'Fowler' McInerney: Won All-Irelands with Clare in 1914 and 1932, and with Dublin in 1927.

1984: Jim Langton: Won All-Irelands with Kilkenny in 1939 and '47. The '47 final was considered a classic when the Cats overcame Cork.

1985: Eugene 'Eudie' Coughlan: Starred for Cork between 1919 and '31, winning four All-Irelands and five Munster titles. Captained Cork to victory in 1931, the year of the 'three finals'.

1986: Tommy Doyle: Thurles star of the Tipperary team from the 1930s to the '50s. Won five All-Irelands and six Munster Championships. Famous for his performances marking Christy Ring.

1987: Christy Moylan: Waterford great, played between 1935 and '49. A member of Waterford's first All-Ireland-winning team, in '48.

1988: Paddy 'Fox' Collins: hurled with Cork in the 1920s and '30s, winning All-Irelands in '29 and again in the '31 epic final with Kilkenny.

1989: Michael John 'Inky' Flaherty: Star for Galway from 1936 to '53, winning a National League in '51 as captain. Came on as a sub when Galway lost the '53 All-Ireland final to Cork. He was also a member of the all-Galway Railway Cup team that beat both Leinster and Munster in 1947. Became a prominent referee and coach, and was a noted boxer.

1990: John Joe 'Goggles' Doyle: Played with Clare from 1926 to '38 and considered one of the greatest never to win an All-Ireland. Won a Munster title in 1932 as captain.

1991: Jackie Power: Famous Limerick dual player who starred for the county between 1935 and '49. Won All-Ireland hurling medals with the great Limerick team in '36 and '40. Father of Kerry football legend Ger Power.

1992: The Rackard brothers, Bobby and Billy: The Rackards were part of the great Wexford team of the 1950s along with their brother Nickey. Bobby and Billy won All-Irelands in '55 and '56, with Billy adding a third in '60.

1993: Pat Stakelum: Tipperary star between 1947 and '57. Won three All-Irelands in a row, captaining the team to glory in '49. Also won six National League medals.

1994: Martin White: The Tullaroan legend won three All-Irelands with Kilkenny in 1932, '33 and '35, as well as six Leinster titles. He celebrated his 100th year in 2009.

– LOCAL RIVALRIES –

A Sky News vox pop with random England fans in Lisbon during Euro 2004 took a turn for the worse when their reporter happened upon an Irish tourist. Asked if he was disappointed at England's loss to Portugal, the man replied: 'Not at all; I'm Irish, I'm from Tipperary.'

Reporter: 'But would you not support England when Ireland are not in the competition?'

Tipperary Man: 'No way.'

Reporter: 'Why not?'

Tipperary Man: 'Eight hundred years of oppression.'

Reporter: 'Is there ever any time you would support England?'

Tipperary Man: 'Maybe if they were playing Kilkenny.'

– TOP CATS –

Kilkenny legend Eddie Keher could end up losing his title as the top scorer in hurling championship history, most likely to his fellow countyman and scoring machine Henry Shefflin. However, his status as one of the game's most outstanding marksman will stand the test of time. Keher scored 36 goals and 415 points in a 50-game career between 1959 and 1977, a whopping 110 points more than the great Christy Ring, who played 14 more championship games in his 23-year intercounty innings. In the 80-minute 1971 final against Tipp, Eddie bagged 2–11, a record that stood until 1989, when Tipp's Nicky English scored 2–12 against Antrim over 70 minutes. Keher's tally of 6–45 points in the 1972 hurling championship is also a record. Wexford hero Nicky Rackard, another of hurling's great forwards, recorded the highest confirmed tally in an intercounty championship game when he scored 7–7 against Antrim in the 1954 All-Ireland semi-final, a game played over 60 minutes. Up until the 1930s, scoring records were rarely kept, though Cork's Andy 'Doric' Buckley was reported by some newspapers to have scored 7–4 in the 'home' final against Kilkenny in 1903.

– KINGDOM EXPORTS –

Given their illustrious history of success in Gaelic football, it's little wonder that other counties have tried to tap into the secrets of Kerry's brilliance by hiring a manager who hails from the Kingdom. Several have tried, all with varying degrees of success.

LIST OF KERRYMEN WHO HAVE MANAGED OTHER COUNTIES

Mick O'Dwyer (Laois, Kildare and Wicklow)

Páidí Ó Sé (Westmeath and Clare)

John O'Keeffe (Limerick and Clare)

Liam Kearns (Laois and Limerick)

John Evans (Tipperary)

Mickey Ned O'Sullivan (Limerick)

Tomás Ó Flatharta (Westmeath)

Not to be outdone, the Dubs have provided their fair share of 'exports' to other counties also.

LIST OF DUBS WHO HAVE MANAGED OTHER COUNTIES

Tommy Carr (Roscommon and Cavan)

Val Andrews (Louth and Cavan)

Paul Bealin (Wexford and Carlow)

Barney Rock (Westmeath)

John O'Leary (Wicklow)

Tommy Lyons (Offaly)

Brian Mullins (Derry)

– COLOUR-BLIND –

When Kerry played Mayo in the All-Ireland football final in 1997, the Kingdom changed the style of their jersey before the final, widening the golden hoop through the middle. Word had it that one of Kerry's leading players was, in fact, colour-blind, so to distinguish the Kerry jersey from the Mayo jersey (same style but green with a red hoop), the shape of the band was changed so that it could be determined without the aid of colour. Whether practical or stylistic, it did the trick as Kerry came out on top, ending their long spell of 11 years in the doldrums.

– THE FIRST 'SEÁN ÓG' OF HURLING –

Hurlers are often portrayed as mythical creatures in Irish literature, warriors who produced such displays of skill and strength as to render them almost inhuman. Could Cúchulainn really puck a ball *ard san aer* and chase after it, grabbing the sliotar before it hit the ground? Did he have the accuracy to drive it straight down that hound's throat?

The passage of time often distorts fact, but there are several hurlers from the late 1800s who drew nationwide acclaim for their on-field heroics. It's not surprising, though, that one of the most notable hurlers in the early days of the GAA was called Seán Óg. James 'Seán Óg' Hanley of Kilfinane, Co. Limerick, took his name from his grandfather, a noted left-handed hurler who practised in the same green fields as his grandson did 50 years later.

According to *Carbery's Annual*:

> At 21 years of age, 'Sean Óg' was a giant of a man, six feet one inch tall, deep-chested and long-limbed. He played successfully in many positions of the field, but centre-back was his best. Many years ago, a much older man than me described to me a great day in 1897 when Kilfinane played St Michael's (Limerick) in the hurling county championship. The match was at Kilmallock, and St Michael's team were memorable for they drove out 20 miles from Limerick City in brakes and four grey horses. In a splendid game Kilfinane won, and Sean Óg was the talk of the countryside, because of his mighty hurling. Kilfinane hit their peak that year and they beat Kilkenny in the All-Ireland final.

If stories of the time are to be believed, like those in *Carbery's Annual*, Hanley had the longest puck of any man at that time: 'His length of delivery was immense – 100 yards or more – one of the longest hitters I ever saw. He was a master hurler, with a smooth easy style. He showed rare judgement and accuracy. His energy and strength were immense.'

Little wonder then that Hanley caught the attention of clubs around the country, and according to the article 'GAA Stars of Yesteryear', quoted in Seamus O'Ceallaigh's 'Great Limerick Athletes', he may well have been at the centre of the first case of 'under-the-table' professionalism in the GAA: 'Seán Óg was widely acclaimed as "the Hurler of the Year". Good offers were made to Seán Óg by Dublin clubs and he was employed in Dublin for some time,' reads the piece. Hanley played with Commercials in Dublin for some time before following the path of a large number of his generation and leaving for England. There he joined the Desmonds club and hurled in another All-Ireland hurling final, this time for London against Tipperary in 1900. He died aged 38 and was buried in Kensal Green Cemetery on 29 August 1915 where 'a beautiful Celtic monument' was raised above his grave. As O'Ceallaigh wrote, 'Hanley of Kilfinane was the greatest hurler of his period – rich in fine hurlers.'

Other notable Seán Ógs in the GAA are Seán Óg Ó Ceallacháin, Seán Óg Ó hAilpín and Seán Óg De Paor. There might even be a team of Seán Ógs. Then, of course, there was Seán Óg Flood, son of Tim Flood, who not only won All-Irelands for Wexford in 1955, '56 and '60, but also won an All-Ireland banjo title and was an All-Ireland champion trainer of sheepdogs. So next time Cork hurling fans break into a strain of 'there's only one Seán Óg' . . . think again.

– TEN MILLION REASONS TO SAY THANKS –

While the Dublin and Meath football rivalry has been one of the most engaging in the GAA over the past 25 years, it has also been the most lucrative. When the sides met in the Leinster Senior Football Championship quarter-final in Croke Park on 3 June 2007, they broke the €10 million barrier for gate receipts generated by this fixture between 1983 (when Seán Boylan took charge of the Royal County) and 2007. They also broke the 1.2 million attendance barrier for the same period, an era marked by tight finishes and a number of high-profile draws. Ironically, on the day this notable landmark was reached, Dublin and Meath, true to form, drew 1–11 to 0–14 and had to replay again a fortnight later.

– THE KICK PASS –

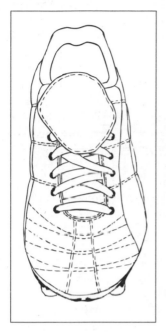

Traditionally, the straight 'punt' kick off the top or the laces of the boot, out of the hand, is the favoured striking action in Gaelic football, but it is really a variation of this action that is most commonly used by expert practitioners. Similar to soccer, there are four fundamental ways of employing the boot to kick a ball, although one of them, the instep, is rarely used in Gaelic except when the ball is played on the ground, 'soccer-style'. A Gaelic football is, of course, heavier than a soccer ball, which ensures a surer flight of the ball in the air for fielding, but it also means that the technique of striking the ball from the hand differs from soccer. While running at pace, most footballers will opt for the straight punt kick when passing to a player directly ahead, using the laces, dropping the ball onto the foot rather than throwing it up. For a right-footed kick, the ball is dropped onto the foot with the right hand. For a left-footed kick, the ball is dropped with the left hand.

The technique of straight punt kicking is often used for goal scoring on the run. However, when going for a point score, the point of contact on the boot shifts more towards the inside to spin the ball, right to left for a right-footed kicker, and left to right for a left-footer. This kick is sometimes referred to as the 'hook kick', and the kicker aims to get plenty of height on the ball. Many coaches often shy away from teaching young players how to use the outside of the boot, but it is a really important action to perfect. A right-footed kicker, for example, will often curl a ball right to left over the bar with the outside of his right boot. A textbook example of this was Maurice Fitzgerald's equaliser against Dublin in the All-Ireland quarter-final in Thurles in 2001, when he curled the ball over the bar from the sideline on the right. For free kicks from the ground, the technique of using the inside of the boot for height and swerve and the laces for power is similar to soccer.

– LOUTH'S MUSICAL HERO –

Music and sport are strange bedfellows, but one man who bridged the gap to become famous for both was Louth's All-Ireland-winning captain in 1957: Dermot O'Brien. O'Brien's talent as a footballer was evident from a young age with the St Mary's club in Ardee, but it was a talent matched by an ability to sing and play the accordion. While playing football with the Louth minors in the early 1950s, he was a member of the Emerald Céilí Band based in Slane, Co. Meath, and was performing all over Ireland, earning a pound a night. He progressed to Louth senior ranks in 1952, but after sustaining a serious injury the following year as the county reached an All-Ireland semi-final with Kerry, he missed a gig with the band and was immediately sacked. Tensions rose between both pursuits, but O'Brien persevered with football, taping his precious fingers together to protect them during games.

Ruled out of action for a lengthy period and sacked from the band, O'Brien used the time to develop his musical talents. However, he was recalled to the Louth panel, and in 1957, he replaced the injured Patsy Coleman as Louth captain for the Leinster final against Dublin. An injection to a shoulder injury nearly cost O'Brien his starting place in the All-Ireland final against Cork. After receiving the jab in a Dublin hotel, he got to Croke Park only to be refused entry by a gateman, ignorant of his identity. A young Garda recognised O'Brien and ushered him through the crowds to the dressing-room with minutes to spare, and he went on to lift the Sam Maguire for the third time in his county's history later that evening.

A broken finger ended O'Brien's football career in 1960, and two years later he became a full-time professional musician, starting up his own band, The Clubmen. He performed extensively to international audiences and had a string of hits, the most famous of which was 'The Merry Ploughboy'. He starred in his own hugely successful television show and appeared on stage with such luminaries as Bing Crosby, Johnny Cash and Bill Haley. Loved as a performer, a gentleman, a fluent Irish-speaker and a wonderful sportsman, he died in 2007 aged 74.

– BEST-KNOWN GAA PUBLICANS –

Páidí Ó Sé: Ard an Bhóthair, Ventry, Kerry

Paddy Cullen: Paddy Cullens (formerly owned), Ballsbridge and Manor Inn Swords, Dublin

Tommy Griffin: Ó Súilleabháins, Dingle, Kerry

Pat Spillane: Pat Spillane's Bar, Templenoe, Kerry

Anthony Daly: Murty Browne's, Tullycrine, Clare

Seán Doherty: Seán Doherty's, Rockbrook, Dublin

Paddy Bawn Brosnan (deceased): Paddy Bawn Brosnan's, Dingle, Kerry

Eamonn 'Ned' Rea: Rea's, Parkgate Street, Dublin

Fran Ryder: Cassidy's, Camden Street, Dublin

Brian Whelahan: Whelahan's, Birr

Larry Tompkins: Larry Tompkins Bar, Lavitts Quay, Cork

Jimmy O'Brien: Jimmy O'Brien's, Killarney, Co. Kerry

– GO GAMES –

The GAA introduced 'Go Games' for juvenile hurlers and footballers in 2004 to help 'maximise participation and optimise playing standards'. The Go Games are structured in such a way as to prioritise the varying development of players and to reduce the potential negative effects of competition at a young age. The basic idea is that every young player will get a 'go' during the game, thereby helping them to develop and increase their enjoyment of hurling and football. There are three levels in Go Games to cater for different age groups: First Touch (age 7–8), Quick Touch (age 9–10) and Smart Touch (age 11–12).

Go Games are initially based on separating the playing area into different zones to encourage players not to stray all over the pitch and to stop powerful players dominating games. It forces children to pass and encourages the development of skills and techniques by issuing points for actions such as blocking. In hurling, striking on the ground is encouraged by not allowing handling of the sliotar for half the game. As the children get a little older, the aims of the Go Games change accordingly to cater for the developing player and help prepare them for the more competitive teenage environment.

– THE RDS AFFAIR –

From 'The Ban' to Rule 42, the GAA has had a somewhat turbulent relationship with soccer down through its history. In recent times, with the opening of Croke Park, attitudes have softened and the competing codes have enjoyed a more harmonious coexistence, but in the past the GAA's wariness of engaging with soccer caused serious controversy. A prime example, and one that drew a clamour of bad press for the Association, came in 1991 when Dublin club Clanna Gael Fontenoy arranged a novel fundraising idea to commemorate their centenary.

The club proposed a challenge game between then All-Ireland champions Down and league winners Dublin to be played as the main event on a double bill with the League of Ireland clash between Bohemians and Shamrock Rovers at the RDS. To the general public, it was an interesting arrangement and one that had the potential to draw large numbers to a unique double-header.

Clanna Gael Fontenoy duly began organising the event, but an intervention from Croke Park scuppered their plans. The GAA's powerful Management Committee overturned the initial decision granting permission for the fixture. It was thought that the committee was against the playing of a GAA match at a non-sanctioned venue. Clanna Gael argued against the objection on those grounds, stating that there were clear precedents, with exhibition matches having been previously staged at grounds such as London's Wembley Stadium and the Toronto SkyDome. The club also maintained that they were bringing Gaelic Games to a part of the capital where it was not traditionally popular – Dublin 4.

The decision attracted a blaze of criticism, with former Clanna Gael chairman Kieran McGinley quitting the Association and lambasting the GAA for its stance, describing it as the 'blackest day in the history of the Gaelic Athletic Association'.

– MORE POWER TO YOU –

One of the defining traits of the GAA is the generational flow of talent down through the years. Brothers lining out alongside each other for club and county is commonplace, while a son following his father's footsteps into the intercounty arena is considered run of the mill. And while there have been many noteworthy and successful tribes, there are few who can boast the geographically diverse success of the late Jackie Power. A renowned exponent of both codes, Power won All-Ireland medals with his native Limerick in 1936 and 1940, and was a member of one of the greatest club hurling sides of all time. Between 1933 and 1939, he won seven consecutive Limerick Championships with Ahane, and then from 1942 to 1948, won seven more.

He gathered his 15th and final Limerick senior medal in 1955 before passing the baton on to his son, Ger, who arguably surpassed the success of his father in the green and gold of Kerry. Ger, one of the central characters on the greatest Kerry team of all time, jointly holds the record for All-Ireland football medals, winning eight in the years between 1975 and 1986.

Jackie, who also hurled for Kerry towards the back-end of his career, had passed away, however, before he got to see a third generation of his family succeed in yet another county. In 1996, Stephen McNamara – grandson to Jackie and nephew to Ger – was part of the Clare team that finally ended 81 years of famine and brought the Liam MacCarthy Cup back to the Banner. McNamara played right corner-forward on Ger Loughnane's team and completed a remarkable three-generation All-Ireland run in three neighbouring Munster counties.

While his on-field legacy lived on, Jackie Power was also commemorated in 1998 when a life-sized bronze portrait of this great sportsman was erected in his native town of Annacotty.

Then you have the case of the Donnellans and the Larkins. Paddy Larkin won All-Irelands with Kilkenny in 1932, '33, '35 and '39, while his son Paddy was on the Liam MacCarthy Cup-winning sides of 1963, '72, '74, '75 and '79. So when his son Philly won his first Celtic Cross in 2000, the generational treble was complete. Similarly, when Michael Donnellan's Galway team won the All-Ireland football title in 1998, he established a record for the family. His father John had already won three All-Irelands, while his Michael's grandfather, also Michael, was part of the victorious Tribesmen team of 1925.

– THE BIG D: THE LYONS' DEN –

Credit for the introduction of an exclusion zone on the edge of the 20-m line of the Gaelic Games pitch is often afforded to Meath's legendary full-back of the 1980s and early 1990s, Mick Lyons. During the last game in the four-game saga against Dublin in 1991, Keith Barr took a penalty for Dublin into the Canal End goal in Croke Park. However, Lyons ran alongside Barr, almost blocking him as he took the kick, which went wide. The penalty was never retaken, but shortly afterwards the GAA introduced an arc on the edge of the 20-m line to exclude players from that area during penalty kicks (pucks) and kick-outs.

– DON'T WORRY –

The history of the GAA is littered with unusually named clubs, but one of the oddest tags ever ascribed to a team was Nil Desperandum. The Cork city outfit came into existence in 1887 on the back of a disbanded, unsuccessful rugby team called Berwick Rangers. After Rangers had folded, some of the lads decided to give the new sport of Gaelic football a try and, given their absence of success on the rugby field, they chose the pithy Latin name Nil Desperandum, translated as 'do not despair', for the club. Nil Desperandum, who became known as 'Nils', actually thrived as Gaelic football blossomed, and they contested the Cork county final in 1891 and won their first crown in 1894.

The following year, they added the Munster title and reached the 1894 All-Ireland final (played in 1895) against Young Irelands of Dublin. The game ended in a controversial draw when the referee was accused of adding enough time for Young Irelands to level matters, a familiar refrain in tight matches to this day. However, the replay three weeks later was even more bizarre. Nils led two minutes from the end of the game when the opposition walked off the field claiming one of their players had been assaulted by a Cork fan. The Nil Desperandum players refused to leave the field, but the referee dithered in his report and referred the matter to the GAA, who ruled that a second replay should take place. Nils refused, and the title was eventually awarded to the Dublin representatives. However, in defiance of the GAA's Central Council and in support of the Cork players, the Cork County Board had a special set of medals struck for the Nils team inscribed 'Nils – All-Ireland Football Champions 1894'.

– GAA GEAR –

Fashion was a late arrival to the world of Gaelic Games. For the first half-century of the GAA, itchy woollen jerseys, knee-length shorts, peak caps and primitive steel-capped boots with leather studs nailed onto the soles were staple attire. Crests on jerseys were something of a rarity, with embellishments usually confined to a sash or a star. Necessity being the mother of invention, players improvised when it came to materials, with items such as flour bags used to make shorts. Jerseys improved after the Second World War as synthetic fabrics became available, but football boots were slow to develop and considered expensive, with the result that many players opted to play in their bare feet or attach strips of leather to the soles of their shoes.

It wasn't until 1970 that the modern O'Neill's leather ball came into use, ending Gaelic football's association with the rain-absorbing pigskin version that grew heavier by the minute on a wet day. While the leather balls were primitive, they were still cherished possessions, and the sack full of footballs is a modern phenomenon. The *camán* stick was also cherished in the past, continually mended and banded, and the helmet didn't appear until the '60s. The arrival of black togs on the Down football team of the '60s was a monumental fashion-leap forward for the GAA. They were also the first GAA team to wear tracksuits. Then, when Dublin exploded onto the scene in 1974 with their exotic navy shorts, the modern era of ever-changing GAA fashion had begun. All of which, of course, invokes the wrath of the ageing GAA traditionalist who laments the passing of the day when men were men, didn't get injured because they cycled everywhere, didn't wear helmets and struck the ball without looking because if you hung on to it, you got thumped. 'When we were young, we used . . .'

– LIGHTNING STRIKES TWICE –

Lightning doesn't strike twice and exotic weather is a rarity for GAA matches in Ireland's temperate climes, before global warming took effect. However, for two Saturday afternoons in a row in August 2008, Croke Park was shrouded in apocalyptic darkness and drenched by freak monsoons. On 9 August, Wexford footballers celebrated a historic victory over Armagh in quite pleasant conditions, but later that day, as Kerry took to the field for the second half against Galway, the skies darkened and the heavens opened. Floodlights were turned on and traffic chaos ensued afterwards when cars had to be abandoned in the rising flood waters. Some people even expected Noah's Ark to sail down Jones's Road. Incredibly, seven days later, Tyrone footballers hammered Dublin in identical conditions with the floodlights brightening a foreboding black sky. Once bitten, twice shy, however, as spectators this time came prepared in oilskins and wading boots. Unfortunately for Dublin fans, the team played as if they too were victims of the plans of the gods.

– ONE HUNDRED AND THIRTY-SEVEN DAYS –

Richie Connor's ill-fated reign as manager of the Offaly senior football team is the shortest in modern GAA history. The 1982 All-Ireland-winning captain lasted just one hundred and thirty-seven days at the helm, overseeing only three competitive matches. Technically, Connor only spent 39 days in charge of Offaly in practical terms as the preceding months constituted the GAA's 'closed season'. However, while his tenure may have been the shortest, Connor's stint wasn't quite as short-lived as Teddy Holland's fleeting period in charge of the Cork senior football team. Holland, a retired Garda, survived 15 days longer than Connor (20 September 2007 to 18 February 2008), but never even got to enter the dressing-room and, after being appointed during a players' strike, the Ballinascarthy man had to resign from his position as one of the conditions required to resolve the conflict.

– GRAVESIDE TRIBUTE TO CHRISTY RING –

Reports estimate that up to 60,000 people lined the streets of Cork for the funeral of hurling legend Christy Ring in March 1979. The graveside oration was delivered by his former teammate and the then Taoiseach Jack Lynch. It included the immortal words:

> As long as young men will match their hurling skills against each other on Ireland's green fields, as long as young boys swing their camáns for the sheer thrill of the feel and the tingle in their fingers of the impact of ash on leather, as long as hurling is played, the story of Christy Ring will be told. And that will be for ever.

– THE TWELVE APOSTLES –

In the tempestuous All-Ireland football final in 1983, four players were sent off: three Dublin players – Brian Mullins, Ray Hazley and Ciaran Duff – and one Galway player – Tomás Tierney. Reduced to 12 men, Dublin made a defiant stand to win 1–10 to 1–8 in a bizarre decider, and the heroic players became known as the 'Twelve Apostles' in the capital. Outside of Dublin, they were afforded a different title, the 'Dirty Dozen', and the game invoked the ire of GAA officialdom and the press, who dubbed it the 'Game of Shame'. The 12 Dublin players who had remained were John O'Leary, Mick Holden, Gerry Hargan, Pat Canavan, Tommy Drumm, P.J. Buckley, Jim Roynane, Barney Rock, Tommy Conroy, John Caffrey, Anton O'Toole and Joe McNally. Dublin made two substitutions, with John Kearns replacing Tommy Conroy and Kieran Maher coming on for John Caffrey.

– HOW TO LIFT A GAELIC FOOTBALL –

– MAGIC MOMENTS –

In 2005, RTÉ television ran a feature on their *Sunday Sport* programme to highlight the Top 20 GAA Moments from the previous 40 years. Viewers were given a chance to vote for a selection of twenty highlights chosen by a panel of ten RTÉ sports personalities, and the programme was presented by managers, former players, broadcasters and officials. The ten judges were myself, Jimmy Magee, Ger Canning, Michael Lyster, Des Cahill, Jim Carney, Brian Carthy, Marty Morrissey, Tony O'Donoghue and Darragh Maloney. There was some surprise with the choice of the top moment by punters. While the GAA pundits accepted Michael Donnellan's run in the All-Ireland final of 1998 was spectacular, they were more inclined towards Seamus Darby's goal for Offaly in the 1982 football final because it changed the course of GAA history. The 20 moments are still viewed regularly by GAA fans on YouTube.

The Top 20 GAA Moments as selected by the viewers were:

1. Michael Donnellan's long solo run for Galway v Kildare in the 1998 All-Ireland Senior Football Championship final.

2. Maurice Fitzgerald's point for Kerry from a sideline kick v Dublin in the 2001 All-Ireland Senior Football Championship quarter-final at Semple Stadium.

3. Seamus Darby's goal for Offaly v Kerry in the 1982 All-Ireland Senior Football Championship final.

4. John Fenton's goal for Cork v Limerick in the Munster Senior Hurling Championship semi-final replay in Thurles.

5. Goalkeeper Davy Fitzgerald's goal for Clare from a penalty for Clare v Limerick in the 1995 Munster Senior Hurling Championship final in Thurles.

6. Kevin Foley's equalising goal for Meath v Dublin in the 1991 Leinster Senior Football Championship first-round third replay at Croke Park.

7. D.J. Carey's point for Kilkenny v Clare in the 2002 All-Ireland Senior Hurling Championship final.

8. Joe Connolly's victory speech for Galway v Limerick in the 1980 All-Ireland Senior Hurling Championship final.

9. Jack O'Shea's goal for Kerry v Offaly in the 1991 All-Ireland Senior Football Championship final.

10. Offaly's comeback v Limerick in the 1994 All-Ireland Senior Hurling Championship final, scoring 2–5 in the last four minutes and fifty-two seconds.

11. Mattie McDonagh's goal v Meath in the 1966 All-Ireland Senior Football Championship final, sealing the three-in-a-row for Galway.

12. Mikey Sheehy's goal for Kerry over the head of Paddy Cullen v Dublin in the 1978 All-Ireland Senior Football Championship final.

13. Michael 'Babs' Keating playing in his bare feet for Tipperary v Kilkenny in the 1971 All-Ireland Senior Hurling Championship final.

14. Peter Canavan's return to the field for Tyrone v Armagh in the 2003 All-Ireland Senior Football Championship final.

15. Jimmy Barry Murphy's goal for Cork v Galway in the 1973 All-Ireland Senior Football Championship final.

16. Eddie Keher's goal for Kilkenny v Cork in the 1972 All-Ireland Senior Hurling Championship final.

17. Paddy Cullen's penalty save for Dublin v Galway in the 1974 All-Ireland Senior Football Championship final.

18. Barney Rock's goal for Dublin v Cork in a 1987 National Football League quarter-final in Croke Park after Cork had left the field.

19. Frank McGuigan's 11 points for Tyrone v Armagh in the 1984 Ulster Senior Football Championship final.

20. Offaly fans' sit-in in Croke Park in 1998 after referee Jimmy Cooney had blown up the All-Ireland Senior Hurling Championship semi-final replay v Clare two minutes early.

– WHISTLE STOP –

One of the most common criticisms levelled at referees, particularly by players, is that they frequently didn't play the game to any notable standard. Not so the great Meath footballer Peter McDermott. McDermott was a corner-forward on the first Meath team to win an All-Ireland in 1949 and captained the county to their second success five years later. In-between, he was on the losing side in two All-Ireland finals – in 1951, when Mayo defeated Meath, and again in 1952, when the Royal County lost out to Cavan in a replay. What is even more remarkable about McDermott is that he refereed the 1953 final between Kerry and Armagh before returning as a player in the decider 12 months later. McDermott also went on to coach Meath to All-Ireland success in 1967 and helped organise the famous Meath tour of Australia in 1968. In 1984, he became the first Irish manager of a Compromise Rules side. Other famous county players to referee at the top level include Sligo's Mickey Kearns, Kildare's Seamus Aldridge, Cavan's Simon Deignan, Cork hurler and former GAA president Con Murphy, Kilkenny hurler Paddy Buggy, Liam Maguire of Cavan, Tommy Daly, Mick Hayes, John Dunne, Bill Delaney and Mick Loftus.

– PINTING THE WAY FOR THE GAA –

The first All-Ireland hurling final took place on 1 April 1888 (the 1887 final) in Birr, Co. Offaly, between the Thurles club, representing Tipperary, and Meelick, representing Galway (the first All-Ireland featuring county selections didn't take place until 1922). The Thurles team were delayed en route to the game and, thinking that the Tipp lads weren't going to arrive at all, the Meelick squad adjourned to the local pub. However, Thurles eventually arrived, and the Meelick boys emerged from the inn and took to the field in their shirts and trousers. One of their crew, John Lowry, actually walked from Killimor to Birr for the game, only to be taken off to balance the numbers after one of the Thurles players had left the field injured. Ignoring his demotion and the ref, Lowry kept returning to the field of play. Thurles took the first All-Ireland hurling crown after scoring 1–1 and a forfeit point as Meelick failed to score at all.

– THE FIVE AGES OF MICK O'DWYER –

KERRY PLAYER: 1956–74

Despite breaking both his legs during his career, Micko played for Kerry from 1956 to 1974, winning four All-Irelands, twelve Munster Championships and seven National Leagues. He was named Texaco Footballer of the Year in 1969 at the age of 33.

KERRY MANAGER: 1975–89

O'Dwyer served as Kerry manager from 1975 to 1989. He won eight All-Irelands (and three under-21 titles), eleven Munster titles and four National Leagues, making him the most successful GAA manager of all time. Micko's championship record as Kerry boss is P55, W43, L7, D3.

KILDARE MANAGER: 1991–4; 1997–2002

Micko caused a sensation in the GAA world when he took charge of Kildare, steering them to the 1991 league final against Dublin in his first season. They contested Leinster finals in 1992 and '93. He resigned in '94, but returned to the job two years later when Kildare finally defeated Dublin in the 1997 Leinster Championship before losing out in a three-game epic with Meath. They were crowned Leinster champions in 1998 but lost the All-Ireland final to Galway. They added another Leinster title in 2000. O'Dwyer stepped down in 2002 after losing the Leinster final to Dublin.

LAOIS MANAGER: 2002–6

After leaving Kildare, Micko took the reins at Laois in the winter of 2002 and steered them to Leinster final glory in 2003, defeating his previous side in the final. It was the county's first Leinster title since 1946. However, he lost the Leinster final the following year to Westmeath, managed by his former charge Páidí Ó Sé.

WICKLOW MANAGER: 2006 TO PRESENT

Micko's trademark enthusiasm has helped revitalise Gaelic football in Wicklow, and the side managed to reach the O'Byrne Cup final in his first weeks of management. In 2008, they won their first Leinster Championship game ever in Croke Park, beating O'Dwyer's former charges Kildare before losing narrowly to Laois. However, Wicklow reached unbelievable levels of ability and endeavour in 2009 by scoring championship wins over Cavan, Fermanagh and Down before losing gallantly to Kildare.

– TRACK AND FIELD –

While the historic 1884 meeting in Hayes's hotel in Thurles is regarded as the pivotal moment in the creation of Gaelic Games, it is also the case that the initial primary concern of the GAA was the reorganisation of athletics and its promotion across all social classes throughout Ireland. In fact, the very first official GAA-sanctioned sports event was an athletics meeting near Macroom in Cork on 11 November, just ten days after the formation of the Association. The founding fathers of the GAA saw an Ireland that had produced some of Europe's finest athletes but also one that excluded or barred many of these from formal competition on the grounds of social or political background.

The GAA immediately set about establishing an athletics programme that was accessible both to nationalists and members of the non-nationalist community. For their part, football, hurling and handball events were often part of the support act for the early major GAA events, which were initially athletics-based, and while the native games were to become the heartbeat of the GAA for over 100 years, they were often omitted from the programme in the early years. There were, according to historians, no intercounty football or hurling matches played in the first 12 months of the GAA's lifespan, though local competitions flourished.

GAA founder Michael Cusack had previously been a member of the Irish Champion Athletic Club, but had left in 1880, and with the wildfire spread of the GAA-organised athletics events, several of his former colleagues took umbrage at the new movement. Many of these founded the Irish Amateur Athletic Association (IAAA), an exclusively non-nationalist organisation which competed with the GAA and held track and field meets of their own for the next 40 years. However, their first major battle with Cusack's new organisation was to prove a fruitless and poignant one in the context of their rivalry with the GAA. In June 1885, the IAAA organised a major event at the County Kerry Amateur Athletic and Cricket Club. Cusack responded by fixing a similar GAA sports day in Tralee. Over 10,000 people showed up in Tralee, while the IAAA event was almost empty.

– KNOW YOUR SQUARE BALL RULE –

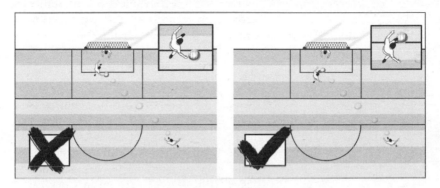

While GAA officials frequently attempt to square the circle when it comes to its rules and their manifold interpretations, they have certainly succeeded in squaring the rectangle when it comes to the square ball ruling. The square ball is the equivalent to soccer's offside rule in that it is generally appealed either way by players and spectators. Depending on your persuasion, the player was either in the square or he wasn't before the ball arrived.

Knowledge of the square ball rule is a 'gimme' for all Gaelic Games aficionados, and it is simply unacceptable to be ignorant of this classic rule first introduced in 1910 when a small parallelogram was created prohibiting players from scoring inside that zone.

According to the GAA's *Official Guide*, the square ball ruling for both hurling and football is identical. It is a technical foul 'for an attacking player to enter opponents' small rectangle before the ball enters it during the play'. However, there are two exceptions:

i. If an attacking player legally enters the small rectangle, and the ball is played from that area but is returned before the attacking player has time to leave the area, provided that he does not play the ball or interfere with the defence, a foul is not committed.

ii. When a point is scored from outside the small rectangle and the ball is sufficiently high to be out of reach of all players, the score shall be allowed even though an attacking player may have been within the small rectangle before the ball – provided that the player in question does not interfere with the defence.

– THE VOICE –

For nearly 50 years, Michael O'Hehir was the voice of Gaelic Games on radio and subsequently on television. From his debut as an 18-year-old commentator in 1938, O'Hehir was the conduit between the Games and the people of Ireland, particularly those in rural Ireland. Before the advent of television, the stars of the game and the epic encounters in Croke Park were painted graphically by O'Hehir's words over the radio. However, it was never the limit of his broadcasting talent. In fact, many of the most famous lines attributed to O'Hehir come from his years commentating on televised games. The All-Ireland football semi-final in 1977 was a case in point. Considered by many to be the greatest game of football of all time, O'Hehir remarked shortly after half-time: 'Twenty-nine minutes still remaining in this game, hallelujah!' Later in the game, Dublin's Bernard Brogan, just back from a stint on an oil rig off the coast of France, scored the crucial goal. O'Hehir described the moment. 'Bernard Brogan drilling for oil . . . he drilled for goal there and drilled right into the back of the net.' While the 'Foinavon' Grand National at Aintree in 1967 is always considered to be his finest moment as a professional commentator, from a GAA perspective that came at the 1947 All-Ireland football final in New York when he prolonged Radio Éireann's broadcast time on the rented lines so that the delayed final could be relayed back to Ireland in its entirety. He did so by pleading live on air to whoever controlled the plug. Afterwards, O'Hehir admitted that from that day on he realised that, as a broadcaster, he was really an ambassador for Gaelic Games.

– TABLE MANNERS –

GAA presidents aren't known for immortalising witty one-liners willy-nilly, but in 2000, Peter Quinn famously broke the mould in some style. Granted, he was at that stage a former president, but it was worth the wait anyway. The context was the controversial issue of payments to intercounty managers, illegal in GAA law. Seán McCague, Quinn's successor in GAA head office, suggested at a Cavan county convention that year that more than half of intercounty managers were receiving sums of money from county boards for their services. He then set up a task force, which Quinn was to chair, but despite some painstaking work and a nationwide hunt for these so-called 'under-the-table' payments, Quinn and his associates came up with a blank. In the document Quinn later submitted to McCague, Quinn not only conceded that he could find no trace of the under-the-table payments, he also admitted, quite amusingly, that 'we couldn't even find the table'.

– PAST PERFECT, PRESENT TENSE –

Most generations of players and supporters are expected to defer to the superiority of previous players and styles; footballers are weaned with tales of the great 'catch and kick' approach of the past, while contemporary hurling never seems to measure up to the historic classics. However, it has always been thus.

Writing in his *Annual* in 1939, the famous hurler and hurling historian P.D. Mehigan, better known as Carbery, commented on the rapid growth of hurling while lamenting the fact that there had been no concurrent improvement in technique and that the 'pure style' of hurling practised in the early part of the twentieth century had been diluted. Contemporary hurlers, Carbery remarked, could not strike a ball as well as the men of Tubberadora, Blackrock, Mooncoin or Tulla. He claimed that the players of 1939 could no longer tackle, sidestep, parry, hook, pull, double, drive or drop a ball on the ground, or connect accurately with a flying 'drop'. The reason for the decline in standards, according to Carbery, was the absence of good instructors and the priority given to speed. Sound familiar?

Kerry football legend and controversial pundit Pat Spillane wasn't quite as eloquent and technical as Carbery. Nearly 70 years later, after his native county had been denied by an incredibly tenacious display by Tyrone in the 2003 All-Ireland football semi-final, Spillane described the Ulster side's tactics as 'puke football'. Tyrone have since then added three All-Irelands, beating Kerry twice in finals with an exciting brand of pass-and-move football orchestrated by astute manager Mickey Harte – a style of football played at breakneck speed.

As in most things in life, the only real constant is change. And for those in their prime, revelling in the stars of today, it won't be long before the children of tomorrow are being lectured on how the likes of Henry Shefflin, Seán Óg Ó hAilpín, Colm Cooper and Peter Canavan will never be seen again. As they say, if you look too much to the past, you'll soon be headed that way. While the basic skills must always be preserved, each generation has the right to play the games as they wish.

– RULES, WHAT RULES? –

The International Rules Series between Ireland and Australia has its roots in a number of informal tours that took place in the late 1960s. Former Aussie Rules umpire and sports broadcaster Harry Beitzel brought an Aussie team to Croke Park to play Mayo and then All-Ireland champions Meath in October 1967. The following year, Beitzel brought an Australian representative outfit on a 'world tour', playing games against GAA teams from Dublin, Meath, Kerry, London and New York. Meath then travelled out to Australia in 1968, where they played five games, winning all five. Kerry followed suit in 1970 with a successful trip Down Under. Eight years later, Beitzel was back in Ireland with a team that played UCD and Kerry, but it wasn't until a number of reciprocal trips between college and schoolboy sides had taken place in the early 1980s that a formal international Compromise Rules Series was arranged between the GAA and the Australian Football League.

The first Test match between the countries took place in October 1984 in a very rough game when Australia defeated Ireland 70–57 in Páirc Uí Chaoimh in front of a crowd of 8,000. The Compromise Rules saw a round ball used, though players could take six steps before having to bounce or solo and could pick it directly off the ground without using the foot. The scoring system saw six points awarded for a normal 'Gaelic football' goal, three points for a normal 'point' and a single point awarded for a 'behind' when the ball travelled between the large post and a smaller post 6.4 m either side of the goal, similar to Aussie Rules. Teams were made up of fifteen players a side, including a goalkeeper, and matches were divided into four quarters. Ireland won the second Test in Croke Park by 80 points to 76.

The third Test match in Croke Park in 1984 drew a crowd of 32,000, and while the visitors claimed a 2–1 series victory, the occasion was marred by a number of nasty brawls. These matches introduced some of the stars of the Aussie game to an Irish audience, with figures such as Robert DiPierdomenico (or 'The Dipper') earning an enduring reputation in Ireland.

Dublin manager Kevin Heffernan led the first successful formal Irish Compromise Rules touring party to Australia in 1986.

While the game was seen as a great platform for Gaelic footballers from low-profile counties, punch-ups were a constant feature. Although many claimed they were the most entertaining aspect of the game, the authorities took a dim view of the brawling, and after Eugene McGee steered Ireland to victory Down Under in 1990, the series was suspended until 1998, when Ireland defeated the visiting Australians. A year later, Ireland retained their crown in Australia with a combined attendance of 109,500 watching the two games.

The series continued to grow in popularity with punters as an annual event in the 2000s, but it wasn't without its critics, and when Graham Geraghty was knocked unconscious during a 2006 Test match in Croke Park in front of 82,000 spectators, the GAA cancelled the 2007 fixtures and threatened to end the series unless steps were taken to eradicate the violence. However, the 2008 visit to Australia passed off without incident, with Ireland claiming their ninth victory over the Aussies. Since the beginning of the series, Ireland led 9–5 overall.

Following the tragic death of Tyrone football captain Cormac McAnallen in 2004, the trophy awarded to the winning International Rules team was named in his honour.

– MANAGERIAL MERRY-GO-ROUND –

Given the haste with which counties hire and fire their managers nowadays, it's interesting to note how often the managerial merry-go-round goes full circle, with leaders returning to their counties for a second and even a third crack at success. However, none of them can compare to Donegal stalwart Brian McEniff, who has had no fewer than five official stints in charge of the county's footballers since first assuming office in 1972.

RETURNING MANAGERS IN THE 'MODERN ERA'

Five Stints

Brian McEniff (Donegal footballers 1972–5, 1976–8, 1980–6, 1990–4, 2003–5)

Three Stints

Mickey Moran (Derry footballers 1980–4, 1995–6, 2003–5)
Johnny Clifford (Cork hurlers 1982–3, 1985–8, 1993–5)

Two Stints

Kevin Heffernan (Dublin footballers 1973–6, 1979–86)

Mick O'Dwyer (Kildare footballers 1991–4, 1998–2002)

Billy Morgan (Cork footballers 1986–96, 2003–7)

John O'Mahony (Mayo footballers 1987–90, 2006 to present)

John Maughan (Mayo footballers 1995–9, 2003–5)

Eamonn Coleman (Derry footballers 1991–4, 1999–2002)

Jack O'Connor (Kerry footballers 2004–06, 2008 to present)

Luke Dempsey (Carlow footballers 2004, 2008 to present)

Michael 'Babs' Keating (Tipperary hurlers 1986–94, 2005–7)

Eamonn Cregan (Limerick hurlers 1986–8, 1997–2002)

Fr Michael O'Brien (Cork hurlers 1983–5, 1989–93)

Cyril Farrell (Galway hurlers 1979–82, 1984–91)

Gerald McCarthy (Cork hurlers 1981–2, 2006–9)

When it comes to managing different counties, however, all of the above are in the ha'penny place when compared to the late Paddy O'Hara. O'Hara began his coaching career as player–manager with Antrim in 1956 and went on to lead no fewer than six counties – all from Ulster – in his lifetime. Incredibly, these periods in charge of two-thirds of all the counties of Ulster came before the advent of decent expenses for managers travelling to training.

MANAGERS ON THE ROAD

Six counties: Paddy O'Hara (Antrim, Fermanagh, Armagh, Derry, Donegal, Down).

Five counties: Mickey Moran (Derry, Sligo, Donegal, Mayo, Leitrim).

Four counties: Mick O'Dwyer (Kerry, Kildare, Laois, Wicklow); John Maughan (Clare, Mayo, Fermanagh, Roscommon).

Three counties: Eamonn Coleman (Derry, Longford, Cavan); John O'Mahony (Mayo, Leitrim, Galway); P.J. Carroll (Leitrim, Cavan, Sligo); Páidí Ó Sé (Kerry, Westmeath, Clare); Luke Dempsey (Westmeath, Carlow, Longford); Mattie Kerrigan (Meath, Westmeath, Cavan); Pat Roe (Carlow, Wexford, Offaly); Tom Carr (Dublin, Roscommon, Cavan).

– MELODY MAKER –

The theme music for RTÉ television's flagship GAA programme *The Sunday Game* is a piece called *Jagariarten* written by veteran German composer, double bassist and big-band leader James Last. The title music has accompanied the programme since it first appeared on RTÉ2 back in 1979. However, in 2004 the station decided to replace the theme with a newly composed piece, provoking a lot of criticism and indifference to the new title music in the process. Another new composition was tried in 2007, but met with the same reaction. In 2008, the programme's producers conceded and a newly arranged version of Last's original theme was reinstated. Last was no doubt flattered that his composition remained entwined with the modern cultural history of the GAA. Still, one wonders if the fact ever even registered with a man who has sold well over 100 million albums.

– FRAXINUS EXCELSIOR –

The native Irish ash tree (*Fraxinus excelsior*), or *crann fuinseoige* in Gaelic, holds an almost mythical place in Irish history. A sacred tree to the ancient druids, the ash was often made into ritualistic wands, and it continues to be the source of magic today in the hands of the great hurlers.

A deciduous tree (it sheds and renews leaves annually), the ash grows quickly up to around 25 m in height and 20 m spread. It also resprouts quickly after being cut down. Although technology is beginning to make synthetic alternatives viable, most hurleys are still usually made out of wood from the ash tree. The wood from the lower part of the trunk – the bottom 1.5 m – is used to make the hurley, as the bend in the grain just above the roots suits the shape of the stick down to the bas (the lower part of the hurley). Using the natural grain of the tree also gives a hurley strength and flexibility. For quality hurleys, the tree should usually be aged between 20 and 30 years before it is felled during the winter, when the sap content is at its lowest. The drier the wood, the less likely the hurley is to warp.

Once hewn, the ash is cut into lengths and left to dry for up to nine months before being shaped using a template, then trimmed and sanded. Metal bands are attached around the lower part of the bas to protect the wood from splitting, while material is also added to improve grip.

While ash is an excellent renewable resource, it still takes time to mature, and the growth in the popularity of hurling continues to test the supply. An acre of ash woodland will produce over 1,500 hurleys, but with demand in Ireland exceeding a quarter of a million sticks each year, makers are forced to import European ash to meet the demand. The scene keeps changing. Some of the hurleys in use in Ireland today are now being made in other countries.

– BLACK IS THE COLOUR –

Sportspeople are often slaves to pre-match superstitions, so it's not surprising that many footballers and hurlers have their own rituals before the commencement of battle. Group superstitions are less common, however, though the Sligo footballers of 2001 did engage in a little hocus-pocus before their All-Ireland qualifier with Dublin in Croke Park. In the previous round, Peter Ford's team had shocked Kildare, a team who share Sligo's predominantly white jersey. Hence, Sligo were forced to change into their reserve strip, a much more threatening black number. Following the dramatic last-gasp victory in Croker, they decided the new gear was a lucky one.

A decision was made to retain the jerseys for the Dublin match back at GAA headquarters two weeks later, but the move brought opposition: not from the Sligo public, but from the GAA itself. The Games Administration Committee informed Sligo that the all-black kit would clash with the referee's attire, and fined the county board. Then chairman Joe Queenan described the situation as 'a case of bureaucracy gone mad'. Either way, Sligo's luck ran out fairly quickly and, despite donning the black, they were beaten by 14 points by the Dubs.

Former Carlow football boss Liam Hayes suggested a much more dramatic way to halt Carlow's poor record in the league and championship, however. He went way beyond Sligo's reversing of colours and suggested that the Barrowsiders abandon their own altogether. Hayes reasoned that coming up with a new set of county colours would banish their bad run of form and result in more pride being shown in a new jersey the players could be proud of.

– ANIMAL FARM –

Michael 'Babs' Keating has long been one of the most endearing characters in the GAA. As a player, he excelled in both codes with distinction for his native Tipperary, winning two All-Ireland hurling championships, four Munster titles, two National League medals, and Railway Cup medals in both codes in an eleven-year career between 1964 and 1975. He also guided the county to a further two Liam MacCarthy Cups in 1989 and 1991 during his first stint as hurling manager. But he's also known for some of his colourful assessments of opposition teams and, at times, his own.

'Part of what makes me what I am is that I say what I think without regard for the consequences. At least I am honest. Diplomacy was never a strong point,' he wrote in his 1996 autobiography, *Babs, a Legend in Irish Sport* – and with just cause. In 1990, perhaps still high on the previous summer's All-Ireland triumph, Babs famously declared, 'You can't win derbies with donkeys,' in reference to the Cork team his Tipp side were about to face in the Munster final. His side lost by 4–16 to 2–14, and the 'donkeys' went on to win the All-Ireland.

Not to be deterred from the animal theme in his new surrounds, Babs castigated his Offaly side of 1998 for their performance in a 3–10 to 1–11 defeat to Kilkenny in that season's Leinster final, labelling them 'sheep in a heap'. Babs resigned after some of the flock protested against his appraisal of their performance, and yes . . . you guessed it . . . the 'sheep' went on to win the All-Ireland.

– IF AT FIRST YOU DON'T SUCCEED, TRY AND TRY AGAIN –

The Wexford County Board hosted one of the most bizarre football championships of all time back in 1884, which Rosslare won by beating Crossabeg in the final. What makes the final so unique in GAA history was the scoreline: Rosslare, three tries; Crossabeg, two.

At the time, both football and hurling were in the early stages of development, and Maurice Davin's rules and playing guides left gaping black holes in the interpretation of how the games should be played. It seems as though in Wexford, where a running game was the norm, they used the number of times a player went over the end line of the opposition as the means of determining a winner in the event of a scoreless draw.

– RECENT ALL-STARS WHO HAVE NEVER WON AN ALL-IRELAND SENIOR FOOTBALL MEDAL –

1. Fergal Byron (Laois)
2. Brian Lacey (Kildare)
3. Paddy Christie (Dublin)
4. Seán Marty Lockhart (Derry)
5. Francie Grehan (Roscommon)
6. Glenn Ryan (Kildare)
7. James Nallen (Mayo)
8. Dermot McCabe (Cavan)
9. Rory O'Connell (Westmeath)
10. Dessie Dolan (Westmeath)
11. Ciarán McDonald (Mayo)
12. Eamonn O'Hara (Sligo)
13. Declan Browne (Tipperary)
14. Colin Corkery (Cork)
15. Matty Forde (Wexford)

– DOUBLE TROUBLE? –

To try or not to try, that is the question. So often in the winter and spring one hears the mantra – 'it's only the league' – when a team gets their season off to a rocky start. Similarly, if a less fancied team racks up an unexpected batch of impressive victories in those formative months, the whisper is that they're peaking too early and will inevitably be drowned by the rising tide of the natural order. So is winning league silverware beneficial or detrimental to a county's chances of climbing the steps of the Hogan Stand come the first or third weekends of September? Well, statistics show that the chances of winning All-Ireland honours in the same year as league success are roughly one in four. Between 1926 and 2008, 19 of 75 hurling league winners have gone on to win the All-Ireland – or 25 per cent. In football, the percentage is only slightly lower, with 17 of 74 counties managing the league and championship double in the same year in that time period – or 23 per cent.

– THEY SAID IT –

'I never retired, they just stopped picking me.'

– Former Derry footballer Tony Scullion

'It was a combination of a number of factors: exhaustion, apprehension and get-me-out-of-here syndrome.'

*– Roscommon manager John Maughan
after a heavy defeat to Meath in 2006*

'Tyrone are the Taliban of Gaelic football.'

*RTÉ pundit Colm O'Rourke getting slightly carried away with
the physical nature of the Red Hands' training regimes*

'I'm always suspicious of games where you're the only ones that play it.'

*– Former Ireland International soccer manager
Jack Charlton on hurling*

'The toughest match I ever heard of was the 1935 All-Ireland semi-final. After six minutes, the ball ricocheted off a post and went into the stand. The pulling continued relentlessly and it was 22 minutes before any of the players noticed the ball was missing.'

– Former Tipp hurler Michael Smith

'My only consolation was that I held Tomás Mannion [Galway's corner-back] scoreless.'

– Joe Brolly on one of his less lethal performances

'There won't be a cow milked in Clare tonight.'

*– Marty Morrissey after Clare's 1992
Munster Championship victory*

'There won't be a cow milked in Finglas tonight.'

*– Keith Barr after Erin's Isle's dramatic 1998
All-Ireland Club semi-final win*

'If Offaly win the National League again this year, it will be the greatest accident since the *Titanic*.'

– Offaly's Paul O'Kelly

'I often wonder if we changed the names of counties and jersey colours and started all over again, would it make a difference?'

– Kevin O'Brien, Wicklow's only All-Star

'They shot the wrong Michael Collins.'

*– Meath's Ollie Murphy shows his
discontent at referee Michael Collins*

'I warned the boys they couldn't go through the league unbeaten, and, unfortunately, they appear to have listened to me.'

*– Former Tyrone manager Art McRory
after losing a league match*

'They had the hurling, and they had the heart. But why wouldn't they: it's bred into them with their mother's milk!'

– Kilkenny stalwart Phil 'Fan' Larkin
on James Stephens and hurling bloodlines

'I didn't mind a fella who wanted to know why or to argue the toss. That was good. He had to understand, though. In the end we'd do it my way.'

Legendary Dublin football manager Kevin Heffernan

'John Hoyne was warming up in the dressing-room and he got a slap of a hurl in the head from someone. He got four staples before he went out. That was just the warm-up.'

– Henry Shefflin illustrates Kilkenny's unique
pre-match routine before the All-Ireland final of 2002.

'For the coming year, the hurling finals are being played in Abu Dhabi. Will this be Yabba-Dabba-Doo for the interprovincials? Maybe Fred Flintstone will get a game.'

– Connacht Secretary vents his dissatisfaction with the GAA's
continued backing of the interprovincial championships

'Under-18 and under-21 grades in camogie in Dublin would halve the city's drink problem in the stroke of a pen.'

Irish Times journalist, camogie fan and coach Tom Humphries

'Keep your eye on the ball, even when it's in the referee's pocket.'

– Christy Ring

'It's memories of matches and fellas you played with that you'll bring to the grave.'

– Iconic Cork hurling goalkeeper Dónal Óg Cusack

– THE WORLD OF THE GAA –

Ireland may be divided into 32 counties, but within the GAA football and hurling intercounty competitions there are a cluster of 'foreign counties'. London, for example, have a rich history of GAA activity, winning an All-Ireland hurling title in 1901 and reaching the football finals of 1901, '02, '03 and '08. Since then, they've competed fruitlessly on the bottom rung of the National Football League and in the Connacht Championship. New York have also fielded a team in the Connacht football championship since 1999, though the closest they've come to an Exile upset was the 2004 meeting with Leitrim when the game went to extra time before their more fancied opponents pulled away for the win. They've also had a degree of hurling success, though the Big Apple's small-ballers have plied their trade only sporadically over the past decade and always in the Ulster hurling championship, where they reached the final against Antrim in 2006.

In 2007, Warwickshire competed for the first time in the bottom tier of the National Hurling League, and in 2009 in the Lory Meagher Cup. In addition, there are also two regional teams who compete in hurling. The 2007 season saw the advent of the Fingal team, which is made up of players from clubs in that heavily populated area of Dublin that, traditionally, hasn't been a hotbed of hurling activity. County Down, too, is segregated for the purposes of promoting hurling. The traditional Down hurling clubs are all located on the Ards Peninsula and compete in the Antrim hurling leagues. In order to give the game a boost in the more football-orientated part of the county, a South Down team was established in 2007. Since then, they've been nicknamed the Non-Ards.

– EARLY ELITE –

Tired of the same old teams winning the All-Ireland every year? Yearn for a seismic shift in the balance of power away from the traditional football and hurling heavyweights? Well, it hasn't always been that way. Far removed from the Tyrone–Kerry axis that currently exists in football, the early years of the game were dominated by Dublin. Backboned by a sort of 'league of nations' team, they won 11 of the first 22 All-Irelands on offer. They won back-to-back All-Irelands in 1891 and '92 and in 1901 and '02, and won three together on the spin between 1897 and '99 and 1906 and '08. Tipp are next in line for 'Team of the 1800s', winning three by the year 1900.

Wexford, from 1915 to '18, became the first team to win four on the trot, and the Model County's run could have been even more impressive had they not lost consecutive finals to Kerry in the two years previous to their historic run. Roscommon (1943 and '44), Cavan (1947 and '48) and Mayo (1950 and '51) all won back-to-back All-Irelands before Down's double in 1960 and '61, and Galway's brilliant team managed to bring three titles west of the Shannon between 1964 and '66 before Offaly won back-to-back All-Irelands in 1971 and '72.

The '70s and '80s are well documented, though the decade with the widest spread of Sam Maguires is the '90s, when no fewer than eight different counties shared the 'canister', as Páidí Ó Sé calls Sam Maguire.

Unfortunately, the hurling championship hasn't ever been as geographically diverse. Dublin, Kerry and London did manage early victories, but between Kilkenny, Cork and Tipperary, the 'big three' have accounted for eighty-six of the one hundred and twenty-one All-Ireland finals played to date.

– THEY USED TO WEAR –

Monaghan: Black and amber (1932–6)

Roscommon: Black and amber or black and white (pre-1943)

Sligo: All black (pre-1925)

Longford: Green and white hoops (pre-1918)

Laois: Black and amber (pre-1932)

Westmeath: Green with white hoop (pre-1912)

Down: Blue with white trim (1923–33)

Armagh: Black and amber (pre-1936)

Kerry: Green and red (pre-1903)

Wicklow: Green (pre-1931)

Cork: Saffron and blue (pre-1919)

– TWENTY GAA GROUNDS
BY OFFICIAL CAPACITY –

1. Croke Park (Dublin): 82,300
2. Semple Stadium (Tipperary): 55,000
3. Gaelic Grounds (Limerick): 50,000
4. Páirc Uí Chaoimh (Cork): 43,000
5. Fitzgerald Stadium (Kerry): 43,000
6. St Tiernach's Park (Monaghan): 36,000
7. McHale Park (Mayo): 35,000
8. Pearse Stadium (Galway): 34,000
9. Casement Park (Antrim): 32,500
10. Páirc Tailteann (Meath): 30,000
11. Nowlan Park (Kilkenny): 30,000
12. Dr Hyde Park (Roscommon): 30,000
13. O'Moore Park (Laois): 27,000
14. Healy Park (Tyrone): 25,000
15. Breffni Park (Cavan): 22,000
16. Celtic Park (Derry): 22,000
17. Dr Cullen Park (Carlow): 21,000
18. Wexford Park (Wexford): 20,000
19. Páirc Esler (Down): 20,000
20. Brewster Park (Fermanagh): 20,000

– SYNTHETIC STICK –

In 2008, Diarmuid Horan of Offaly hurling fame became the first player to play a Senior Intercounty Championship match with a synthetic hurley. Horan lined out for the Faithful County against Laois in the opening round of the Leinster Hurling Championship using a stick made completely from synthetic materials. The hurley, produced after six years of research, is designed and manufactured by Cúltec, a Ferbane-based company, and claims to have 'all the positive characteristics of an ash hurley but without any of its limitations'.

– FIVE HOURS AND FORTY MINUTES –

KEVIN FOLEY'S GOAL V DUBLIN, 6 JULY 1991

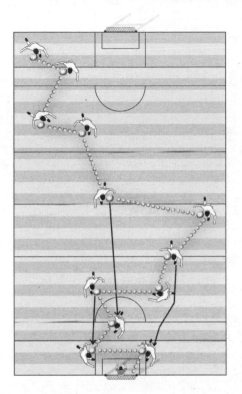

The four-game Leinster football championship saga between Dublin and Seán Boylan's Meath in 1991 was remarkable for many reasons. It wasn't the longest-running sequence of draws; pride of place there goes to the Connacht football championship clash between Sligo and Roscommon in 1925, which took six matches to decide. But the Meath–Dublin affair was significant on a number of levels, none more so than the fact that it really captured the sport at its most appealing. A bitter rivalry had developed between the two counties over the previous ten years, intensifying with Meath's Leinster dominance from 1986 to '91, albeit with a blip in '89, when Dublin prevailed. Games were tight, physical affairs frequently punctuated by mass brawls, to the delight of the watching crowds and the dismay of the authorities. Both sides included a number of iconic players who were tough and uncompromising, men such as Liam Harnan, Mick Lyons, Martin O'Connell and Robbie O'Malley for Meath, and Keith Barr, Eamon Heery, Mick Kennedy and Tommy Carr for Dublin.

However, while the authorities might have frowned on the punch-ups, they had a lot to be thankful for as the profile of the 1991 series between Dublin and Meath re-established the position of Gaelic Games in the wake of the success of the Irish soccer team. Over two hundred and forty thousand fans attended the four matches in Croke Park, and the gripping final instalment was televised live. The games were extraordinary in the manner in which they swung, but the climax on Saturday, 6 July left the nation enthralled. Dublin, managed by 1970s goalkeeper Paddy Cullen, led by three points with a minute remaining of normal time when Meath worked the ball the entire length of the field through eleven passes without a Dublin player touching the ball to equalise with a goal from defender Kevin Foley. To add to the romance of the occasion, it was the only goal Foley ever scored for club or county, before or since. Then, as another draw looked likely, a great cross-field pass by Liam Hayes to P.J. Gillic was fed to David 'Jinxy' Beggy, who fired the winning point. Dublin had one last chance to salvage a draw, but Jack Sheedy's long-range effort curled wide at the Canal End. At the time, I commented that I had never seen a finale like it.

Sadly for Meath, their achievement was not capped with an All-Ireland title as Down burst onto the scene to take the Sam Maguire later that year, despite the heroic efforts of Colm O'Rourke, who defied illness to play. But the saga is etched into the memories of the Gaelic football fans who witnessed the five hours and forty minutes of some of the most engaging drama ever witnessed at GAA HQ.

LEINSTER SENIOR FOOTBALL CHAMPIONSHIP 1991, PRELIMINARY ROUND

Prelim Rnd	Meath 1–12	Dublin 1–12
Replay 1	Meath 1–11	Dublin 1–11 AET
Replay 2	Meath 2–11	Dublin 1–14 AET
Replay 3	Meath 2–10	Dublin 0–15

– GAA POLITICS –

The following is a list of GAA TDs by political party.

FIANNA FÁIL

Tony Dempsey: Former Wexford hurling manager
Liam Lawlor: Former Dublin hurler
Jack Lynch: Former Cork hurler
Hugh Gibbons: Former Roscommon footballer
John Wilson: Former Cavan footballer
Des Foley: Former Dublin footballer and hurler
Seán Brosnan: Kerry footballer
Seán Flanagan: Mayo footballer
Mick Herbert: Limerick hurler
Bill Loughnane: Clare and Dublin hurler

FINE GAEL

John Donnellan: Former Galway footballer
John O'Mahony: Former Galway, Leitrim and Mayo manager
Jimmy Deenihan: Former Kerry footballer
Henry Kenny: Former Mayo footballer

LABOUR

Dan Spring: Former Kerry footballer
Brendan Corish: Former Wexford footballer
Dick Spring: Kerry footballer and hurler

SINN FÉIN

Austin Stack: Kerry footballer

INDEPENDENTS

Jack McQuillan: Roscommon footballer
Tom O'Reilly: Cavan footballer

– OUT OF AFRICA –

The GAA's political past can be illustrated in the names of clubs across the country, with a massive number bearing the name of Irish patriots of the past. Yet such was the spite and ill-feeling towards the ruling British at the time, it seemed the GAA would take the side of anyone engaged in struggle with the British Empire just to rub their noses in it. A novel illustration of this was seen when two clubs (one in Tipperary and one in Galway) sprang up at roughly the same time, around the start of the 1900s, with the unusual name 'De Wets'. De Wet referred to Christiaan Rudolf de Wet, the leader of the Boers in South Africa, who were locked in battle with the British in what is commonly referred to now as the 'Second Boer War'. A club called Galway 'Krugers' played in the All-Ireland final of 1900.

– MANAGER OF THE MATCH –

The *Sunday Game*'s annual All-Ireland finals Man of the Match awards are a source of great interest amongst viewers of the programme, with RTÉ delaying the naming of their star man in both the hurling and football finals until their flagship evening highlights programme live from the hotel of the winning team. Most years, the identity of the recipient is hotly debated, with bookies offering odds on which of the players will pick up the prestigious gong. But after the 2008 All-Ireland hurling final, there was something of a fudge among the selection committee after Kilkenny's awesome 3–30 to 1–13 hammering of Waterford. Any number of the Cats had put in potential Man of the Match displays, so instead of choosing one sole winner, RTÉ decided to present the award to Kilkenny manager Brian Cody in recognition for his team's all-round incredible display. Cue some mild outrage from punters who had bet on one of the Kilkenny players to win the award and felt cheated by the decision to give it to Cody, on whom, understandably, no odds had been offered. However, some of the more fair-minded bookies came to their aid and decided in their generosity to refund all losing bets on the result.

– POINTING THE WAY –

The origin of the term 'point' in Gaelic Games is attributed to founding member Maurice Davin, author of the early rules of football and hurling. In 1884, when the games were just beginning to take shape, only goals were considered valid and there was growing concern that too many matches were finishing scoreless. Davin attended one such hurling match between Athenry and Nenagh, but was quoted afterwards as saying the Tipperary side should have been crowned victors on the basis that they 'had hit the ball over the crossbar, Galway having gained no point'. Thereafter 'overs' began to be officially counted as what we now term 'points', though initially they were only tallied in the event that teams had finished level on goals.

– AN OLD CUSTOM –

The Tipperary footballers were caught on the hop back in 1889 when they showed up to their Munster final without a ball. During those scattered times in the GAA, an old rule was still in place whereby both teams produced a match ball – one to be used in the first half and the other in the second. Trailing by six points at the break after using the Cork ball, the Rebels demanded that Tipp produce their one for the second half, knowing full well that they were unable to as the ball had been burst during the warm-up. According to local sources, Cork did, however, agree to play a replay the following week back in Cork, although there was a disagreement over whether just the second half would be restaged or the entire game. Trailing by four points after the short whistle, Tipp insisted that the aggregate scores over the two disjointed halves be used to determine the winner (that is, Tipp) and refused to play on. Cue yet another re-fixture – much to the annoyance of the Tipperary players, of whom at least a dozen are said to have declined to play for a third week in succession – and hence, an easy win for Cork.

– COLD FEET –

From white boots to ashguards, match-day gear has changed drastically down through the generations. Hurling helmets, for instance, have evolved from leather caps into the high-tech, ultra-safe versions used by players today, and have gone from being a matter of choice to being compulsory in 2009. The invention of the ashguard in the mid-'90s created quite a stir also. A hurling glove designed to prevent hand injury, the ashguard immediately became popular with hurlers at all ages and levels, particularly when such notable players as D.J. Carey began wearing one on each hand. Perhaps the most famous example of unique apparel, or lack of, in the GAA was that of the Tulla players who represented Clare in the All-Ireland hurling final of 1889. For reasons unknown, Tulla played the match against Kickhams of Dublin in their bare feet. The game was played in Inchicore with roughly 1,500 in attendance, and torrential rain made the playing surface so slippery that sawdust was spread over the pitch to keep players from falling. Their lack of footwear worked against them, though, and Dublin won by 5–1 to 1–6.

– FOOT AND MOUTH –

World wars, civil wars and the War of Independence have failed to halt the playing of Gaelic Games over the last 125 years, though an unusual outbreak of an animal disease caused the calendar to shut down altogether in 2001. A sheep from a flock in Jenkinstown, Co. Louth, in March 2001 was found to have contracted foot-and-mouth disease. Though not easily contracted by humans, the highly contagious virus is lethal for animals and the outbreak had the potential to devastate Ireland's important export industries of meat and dairy produce. The infected herd was slaughtered, while police were called into action to cull wild animals capable of spreading the disease. A panic engulfed the country and sports fixtures were cancelled. With the National Football and Hurling Leagues only just up and running, teams were forced to sit idly by while the mess was being cleaned up. Challenge matches were fixed on the sly, though, as managers became worried about the lack of match practice in advance of the championship, while the traditional St Patrick's Day All-Ireland club finals were played on 16 April.

Then, that same month, another suspected case of foot-and-mouth disease was found in Tyrone, and an exclusion zone was put around some of the counties in Ulster, causing havoc yet again. Derry, a county through which the zone ran, were forced to play hurling and football league games without those players who resided within the affected area. It did work to the benefit of one team, though. Wexford refused to travel to Newry to play Down in their Division 2B clash and conceded the points. As a result, Down were crowned winners.

– TALE OF WOE –

Sometimes one wonders whether scores of Mayo footballers may have unintentionally walked under ladders at some time in their past or, unbeknownst to themselves, have been born on Friday the 13th. In modern football, no county has endured the same bad luck. Mayo are the quintessential September bridesmaids.

In the past twenty years, they have appeared in no fewer than fourteen All-Ireland finals, winning just one. That depressing statistic for the Connacht men includes senior, under-21 and minor grades. Taking into account that three of those games were replays, they've had seventeen matches in All-Ireland finals and won just one single decider. Since 1989, the green-and-red jersey has graced Croke Park on the third Sunday in September on five occasions: 1989, 1996, 1997, 2004 and 2006, with nothing but repeated heartbreak to show for their efforts.

Mayo's minors have also struggled on the same day. In 2008, they lost to Tyrone after a replay to make it five losses out of five in the past twenty years, while the under-21s are the only ones to buck the losing trend. In 2006, Mayo finally got their hands on an All-Ireland trophy when they beat Cork to clinch the under-21 championship, though it had come off the back of final defeats in 1994, 1995 and 2001.

As for the unluckiest player award, well, there can't be anyone with more runner-up medals than David Brady. He was on the losing end of All-Ireland senior finals in 1996, 1997, 2004 and 2006; the under-21 teams that were beaten in consecutive deciders in 1994 and 1995; and the Ballina side that lost the All-Ireland club final to Crossmaglen in 1999. That's seven losing All-Ireland finals. Brady did finally get to climb the steps of the Hogan Stand, though, when Ballina won the club decider in 2005.

– GAA: BETTER THAN SOCCER? –

Gaelic Games faced really stiff competition again on the national stage in the late 1980s when the Jack Charlton era introduced a period of soccer-mania in Ireland in the wake of Italia '90. However, the four-game saga between Dublin and Meath in the Leinster football championship in 1991 is credited with re-establishing Gaelic Games in the greater public consciousness, while the emergence of Clare as All-Ireland hurling champions in 1995 kick-started a really engaging era of hurling. As live television coverage of Gaelic Games grew significantly so did its popularity. The success of northern counties in the 1990s and the subsequent cessation of the Troubles in the Six Counties also led to a huge growth in Gaelic Games across the border, reflected in the further successes of Armagh and Tyrone in the 2000s.

The upshot of that growth in popularity is that today GAA clubs dominate the sporting landscape in cities and towns all over Ireland. The growth of the GAA club in the community has been, quite simply, phenomenal, as has the burgeoning appeal and commercial success of intercounty competitions. The urban–rural GAA divide has been well and truly bridged, and, in reality, soccer and Gaelic Games now coexist successfully despite the traditional rivalry. Officials still continue to highlight the GAA's apparent weakness in working-class areas of Dublin, but other sports seem somewhat bemused by an organisation as powerful and successful as the GAA constantly feeling under threat.

So there you have it. There is absolutely no reason nowadays to reference soccer in the context of hurling and Gaelic football. None, unless perhaps you suffer from a lingering inferiority complex, or even a postcolonial inferiority complex, in which case we should probably hand over to a psychologist.

– GAELIC GROUNDS –

The largest attendance for a game outside of Croke Park remains the 1961 Munster hurling final between Cork and Tipperary, when 60,177 people packed into the Gaelic Grounds in Limerick. That figure is the official attendance, but it was estimated that another 10,000 bounded the walls and took their place in the stadium without paying, while the turnstile gates were broken due to the volume of late arrivals. Though generally considered underused due to the number of large stadia in Munster (such as Semple Stadium, Páirc Uí Chaoimh and Fitzgerald Stadium), the Gaelic Grounds holds the honour of being just one of three venues outside Croke Park to host an International Rules Test (2009) between Ireland and Australia, after Páirc Uí Chaoimh (1984) and Pearse Stadium in Galway (2007).

– DID ANYONE BRING A FOOTBALL? –

While the growth and development of the GAA was quite remarkable, the early years of competition were somewhat haphazard, with games often ending in disarray and confusion. County competition commenced in 1887, but was suspended in 1888 due to the American 'Invasion' when GAA athletes and hurlers travelled to the USA. However, the third year of competition proper, 1890, was something of an *annus horribilis* for the Association. The Leinster football championship match between Wexford and Kilkenny in Waterford was delayed for hours when referee Dan Fraher realised there wasn't a football in the ground and had to send someone to the town to buy one. By the time the game was completed, at 7 p.m., many of the Wexford fans had missed the boat back to New Ross. The Munster football final the same year between Kerry and Cork ended three minutes early because the ball burst and a replacement couldn't be found as Kerry had not brought a ball. The All-Ireland hurling final in 1890 between Wexford and Cork also ended in disarray after the Cork skipper Dan Lane ordered his players off the field, claiming that Wexford's play was excessively rough. Wexford were leading 2-2 to 1-6 at a time when a goal exceeded any number of points. However, Cork, represented by the Aghabullogue club, were eventually awarded the title.

– OLD AS THE HILLS –

Fraher Field (or Dan Fraher's Field, to give it its original title) in Dungarvan is the oldest GAA ground still in use, dating back to the foundation of the Association. Owned by the Waterford County Board, the ground boasts a 15,000 capacity, and though matches are staged less frequently at the old venue due to the development of Walsh Park in Waterford city, it holds the distinction of hosting the highest number of All-Ireland finals outside of Croke Park. The hurling deciders of 1903, 1905, 1907 and 1911 were all played there; and for the record, Kilkenny won three of those finals, while Cork are the only other county to take top honours in Fraher Field, winning their All-Ireland final against London in 1903.

– WHO DARES SPEAK OF '98? –

'It was as intense and as close to hatred as you could possibly get between two counties.'

– Fergal Hartley, Waterford hurler, on the controversial Munster hurling final replay with Clare of 1998

'The statement was that you hadn't Offaly beaten until the *Sunday Game* was over.'

– Offaly hurler Johnny Pilkington on the twist of fate that saw the Faithful County granted a replay to the 1998 All-Ireland hurling semi-final after referee Jimmy Cooney unwittingly blew the match up two minutes early

'We were looking out the window at all the Offaly supporters sitting on the field. Johnny Pilkington was having a fag, and he said: "Wouldn't you think they'd go off for an auld drink?"'

– Clare hurling captain Anthony Daly as he surveyed the sit-down protest adopted by a massive portion of Offaly supporters at the end of the 1998 All-Ireland hurling semi-final

– SAFE AS HOUSES –

Given the size of attendances at major GAA games over the past 50 years, the Association can boast a remarkable record when it comes to spectator safety. The largest recorded attendance for an All-Ireland final is the 1961 decider, when 90,556 packed into the Jones's Road venue to see Down and Offaly battle it out for the football title. However, some of the official attendance figures in the past may not have done full justice to the actual size of the crowds. Up until 1966, when the lower Cusack Stand was eventually seated, well over half of those present were standing on terraces, a practice that was eventually curtailed in stadia across the world because of major tragedies that occurred at soccer matches in the 1970s and '80s.

With crowds on a par with major international sporting events, it is a testament to both the Association and GAA supporters that they have never suffered any major disasters and have never had to deal with regular crowd trouble on any significant scale.

However, there have been a few incidents in recent memory where things have got somewhat out of hand. The new Páirc Uí Chaoimh in Cork, unveiled in all its glory in 1976, hosted a less than auspicious inaugural Munster football final that year when, after serious overcrowding, the surplus spectators had to be accommodated around the side of the pitch, just feet from the Kerry and Cork players. The game finished in a tense draw, but the replay, which also took place in Páirc Uí Chaoimh, passed off without incident, with the crowd safely billeted behind the wire.

The ill-tempered 1983 All-Ireland football final between Dublin and Galway has gone down in history because of the fractious on-field clashes. However, it is also remembered by Dublin fans present on Hill 16 that day because of the quite frightening overcrowding that occurred when a number of fans arrived late and breached the gates. With little or no room left on the terrace, fans continued to push their way up the old grass verge behind the steps. People fainted due to the pressure, and some stricken supporters were passed over the heads of the crowd to medical crews outside. Still in the era of barbed wire fences, there was no easy exit from the Hill, and the scene was extremely tense, particularly over at the 'toilet' side of the terrace, where Dublin's most vocal supporters traditionally congregated. However, as the match progressed, the Hill eventually settled down, with the section behind thinning out. The terrace was made all-ticket the following year and was redeveloped later in the decade before being completely revamped in 2004.

Despite the recent redevelopment of Croke Park, the GAA decided to hang on to the terracing at the Railway End to ensure a low-cost entry option for fans, but crowd volumes and entry are now strictly controlled and monitored. Strangely, the same applies to the Veltins-Arena in Gelsenkirchen, the home of the German club Schalbe 04. I was there recently, and on a guided tour of the stadium I enquired as to why one of the stands remained terraced. 'Fan culture,' I was told.

– ROPEY GOAL –

You've heard of jumpers for goalposts? Well, how about length of rope for a crossbar? Back in 1892, Cavan Slashers arrived at Armagh Harps' grounds for their Ulster football final replay only to be told that they were to erect their own goalposts. After planting the two side posts into the ground, they found that there was no crossbar to be found anywhere, so they tied a length of rope from one post to the other and used it for the entire match.

– THE SLIOTAR –

The sliotar has had a rich and varied history as the ball for the ancient game of hurling. Materials such as wood, rope, hollow bronze and animal hair were all used at some point in the past to make sliotars, and the ancient Irish Brehon laws, which date back to the seventh century, mention that compensation would be available for anyone killed or injured by a sliotar. The most famous historical reference occurs in the legend of Cúchulainn, when the young warrior Setanta slays the Hound of Culann at King Conor's banquet with a shot from his hurley and ball.

While the weight and size of the sliotar has altered over the past 100 years, the design of the modern sliotar we know today was created by Limerick man Johnny McAuliffe early in the twentieth century. And while there are a number of ways to make sliotars, the most common suppliers today still use McAuliffe's basic design: a centre made of cork, wrapped in yarn, dipped in latex and covered with two pieces of leather sewn together around the sliotar.

Before the development of the modern sliotar, the ball was heavy and wasn't water resistant. During the formative years of the GAA, the sliotar weighed over 300 g, nearly three times what it weighs now. Two standard sizes of sliotar are used today: size 5 for senior hurling (weighing 100–30 g, 23–5 cm in circumference) and size 4 for camogie (weighing 90–110 g, 21 cm in circumference). Oversized soft balls are also used for underage coaching.

– SCÓR –

While primarily a sporting organisation, the GAA takes its cultural remit very seriously and enjoys a rich history of music and song. There had been no formal stage given to the non-sporting side of the GAA in the first 80 or so years of the Association's existence, but that changed in 1969. Rule 4 of the GAA's *Official Guide* states that 'the Association shall actively support the Irish language, traditional Irish dancing, music, song and other aspects of Irish culture'. With that in mind, the GAA introduced a new competition called Scór in 1969 that gave its members the chance to showcase their musical talents, putting on displays in competition form. Scór na nÓg gives the younger GAA members their chance to claim a national title, while Scór Sinsear affords adult GAA members the same opportunity.

Scór na nÓg competitors must be under 17 years of age. There are regional competitions in both competitions and then a national final. There are eight different sections to Scór: *aithriseoireacht* (storytelling), *tráth na gceist* (table quiz), *nuaschleas* (novelty act), *rince fóirne* (group dancing), *rince seit* (set dancing), *ceol uirlise* (instrumental), *bailéad ghrúpa* (ballad group) and *amhránaíocht aonair* (solo singing).

While the profile of Scór may not be quite on the same level as its sporting equivalent, it does have its supporters. Former Armagh captain and ambitious administrator Jarlath Burns wrote recently, 'Without Scór, what have we but another bland sporting organisation?'

Traditionally, All-Ireland final day in Croke Park has been associated with Irish traditional music and exhibitions of set dancing in the middle of the pitch. Irish traditional music notables Frankie Gavin (fiddle), Liam O'Connor (accordion) and Finbar Furey are among those who have performed to the expectant crowd on the first or third Sunday of September.

– PISEÓGS –

Superstitions are not uncommon in the GAA, though the most famous one by far was the 'curse' supposedly put on the Clare hurling team by Biddy Early, a traditional healer from the county. Born in 1798 and christened Brigid Ellen Connors, Early, who took her mother's maiden name, gained notoriety in the area for defying the wishes of the local clergy. She died in poverty in 1874, having married four times; her fourth and final husband, Thomas Meaney, was forty years younger when they tied the knot. The 'curse of Biddy Early' was often pointed to as a paranormal reason for the Banner County's inability to win a second All-Ireland hurling title after 1914, but things came to a head in 1995 when Ger Loughnane's men finally bridged an 81-year gap and brought the Liam MacCarthy Cup back to the people of Clare.

Clare aren't the only team with a curse, however. In Mayo, some locals relate a similar tale of a spell put on the local footballers by a member of the clergy. Versions differ according to the source, but there are three main plotlines as to why Fr Joseph Foy put a spell on the team (which, as it happens, haven't won a senior All-Ireland since 1951):

1. The priest frowned upon Mayo footballers leaving Mass early for a match.

2. He was angered by the actions of one of the squad in the early 1900s, who left for America after impregnating a local girl.

3. The panel ignored his requests for a lift on the way home from Mass.

Piseógs (superstitions) run deep through the fault lines of Kerry football also. Kingdom legend Páidí Ó Sé had the celebrated photographer Colman Doyle visit him the week before the final in keeping with his winning tradition. His former boss Mick O'Dwyer was similarly inclined. When Páidí came face to face with Micko in the 1998 All-Ireland semi-final between Kerry and Kildare, Ó Sé was aware of Dwyer's superstitious preference for the dugout closest to the Canal End in Croke Park, so he stole a march on Kildare by claiming it for Kerry. However, Kildare won the game, so Micko decided to opt for the dugout at the Hill 16 end for the final against Galway, which they lost. So much for *piseógs*.

– WEXFORD ON THE ROPES –

When the Wexford club Blues and Whites were preparing to represent their county against Kerry in the All-Ireland football final in 1914, they were trained for the decider by former Wexford footballer and heavyweight boxer Jem Roche. Jem, a blacksmith by trade, actually fought for the World Heavyweight Championship title against American champion Tommy Burns from Canada in Dublin's Theatre Royal on St Patrick's Day, 1908. Hopes were high for Roche, but unfortunately for the Irish champion, Burns made short work of him, knocking the Wexford man out in less than a minute and a half with a short hook to the jaw. The fight was for a purse of $7,500, but it was also reported that the confident Burns had a substantial side bet on himself at odds of 1 to 3. Wexford also lost to Kerry in a replay in 1914, but made up for the setback by winning the next four All-Irelands on the trot, the first four-in-a-row in GAA history.

– WHAT'S THE POINT? –

The only scoreless draw ever recorded in a senior intercounty competition was the 1890 Munster football final between Cork and Kerry at the Market Field in Limerick. With the sides still scoreless, the game was blown up three minutes early because the ball had burst. The referee declared a draw. Cork won the replay and went on to win the All-Ireland.

– KERRY'S BARREN YEARS –

Since 1903, Kerry have been the dominant force in Gaelic football, winning a massive 35 All-Irelands, 13 more than their closest rivals, Dublin. Following their 1958 triumph, Dublin have only added another six All-Irelands; Kerry, on the other hand, won the title in 1959 and have since claimed the Sam Maguire Cup a further sixteen times up to 2008.

However, after dominating in the 1970s and '80s, Kerry failed to land an All-Ireland for 11 years, between 1986 and 1997, until Páidí Ó Sé guided them back to the top. It was the longest barren spell the county had known since 1903.

1987: After losing a National League final to Dublin earlier in the season, All-Ireland champions Kerry finally surrender their Munster crown to Billy Morgan's Cork in a replay in Killarney, 0–13 to 1–5. Mikey Sheehy and Seánie Walsh retire afterwards.

1988: Páidí Ó Sé, Ger Power, Ogie Moran and Bomber Liston are all on the bench for the Munster final. A young Maurice Fitzgerald franks his arrival on the big stage with a dazzling display, but Kerry go down by a point to Cork, 1–14 to 0–16.

1989: Páidí Ó Sé joins the list of retirees in Kerry as Cork complete a three-in-a-row in Munster, 1–12 to 1–9. Mick O'Dwyer, the most successful Gaelic football manager of all time, retires in the wake of the defeat. He is replaced by Mickey Ned O'Sullivan, one of his charges from the 1970s.

1990: Mickey Ned sends out a new-look Kerry team, but they suffer their worst Munster final defeat ever to Cork – a 15-point rout, 2–23 to 1–11.

1991: After defeating Cork in the Munster semi-final, Kerry arrest the slide temporarily by reclaiming the provincial title with a two-point victory over Limerick. However, the reprieve for Mickey Ned is short-lived as Down, Kerry's old nemesis, defeat them 2–9 to 0–8 in the All-Ireland semi-final following two goals from Peter Withnell. The Ulster champions go on to beat Meath in the final.

1992: Another Munster Championship victory over Cork suggests the rebuilding process is advancing. However, the Kingdom is rocked to its foundations as Kerry crash out to John Maughan's Clare in the Munster final. It marks the end of the road for Mickey Ned, who is replaced by Ogie Moran, another legend from the golden years. Ogie defeats Páidí Ó Sé, minor manager Séamus Mac Gearailt and Con Riordan to land the job. Páidí is appointed under-21 manager.

1993: Ogie Moran brings Bomber Liston out of retirement, but his side fail to reach the Munster final, crashing out to Cork. Kerry under-21s reach the All-Ireland final, but lose by a point to Meath.

1994: Kerry fail to reach the Munster final again as Cork reassert their control over the province. Pressure starts to rise on Ogie and he receives some criticism from former players.

1995: After a blistering start to the Munster final in Killarney, Kerry are eventually worn down by the Rebels, who land their third provincial title on the trot. Ogie Moran's tenure ends as Páidí's side defeat Mayo in a replay to take the All-Ireland under-21 title. Páidí takes the job as senior manager along with selectors Séamus Mac Gearailt, Bernie O'Callaghan, Tom O'Connor and Jack O'Connor.

1996: Kerry defeat Cork 0–14 to 0–11 to win back the Munster title, but are narrowly beaten by Mayo in the All-Ireland semi-final. Páidí is heavily criticised in wake of defeat.

1997: Kerry, now backboned by the successful under-21 side, win the National League, defeating Cork in the final in Páirc Uí Chaoimh. After overcoming Clare in the Munster final, Kerry edge past Cavan in a historic All-Ireland semi-final, 50 years after the sides had met in the Polo Grounds in New York. A young Mike Frank Russell seals the win with a wonderful goal. Despite losing Billy O'Shea to a broken leg early in the final with Mayo, an outstanding display by Maurice Fitzgerald ensures victory for Kerry, 0–13 to 1–7. The barren spell ends.

– A DAMN GOOD THRASHING –

Hurling wouldn't be the strongest sport in the county of Kildare, although they have won a number of junior, senior B and intermediate All-Irelands. However, the Lilywhites hold the dubious honour of enduring the greatest pasting in a senior competitive match when they were annihilated 14–15 to 1–1 by Wexford in a Dr Croke Cup hurling game in 1897: the biggest thrashing on record. The biggest winning margin ever recorded in a Senior Hurling Championship match was Offaly's 10–23 to 0–0 victory over Louth in the 1910 Leinster Senior Hurling Championship. One of the most famous hidings dished out in a Senior Football Championship game was Kerry's destruction of Clare by 9–21 to 1–9 in a Munster Senior Football Championship game played in the west Clare village of Miltown Malbay on 1 July 1979. The game became known as the 'Miltown Massacre'. Kerry went on to win the All-Ireland that year, the second leg of their four-in-a-row.

– BANDS OF BROTHERS –

Whether nature or nurture, the tradition of the family in Gaelic Games is a rich one and continues to thrive today. Many of the greatest club and county sides have been backboned by brothers, frequently carrying the torch for their forebears, and a number of family names enjoy a privileged place in the history of the games.

The Doyles of Mooncoin, for example – Dick, Eddie and Mick – amassed 18 All-Ireland hurling medals between them playing with Kilkenny in the early decades of the twentieth century. More recently, the Spillane brothers – Pat, Tom and Mick – went one better, bagging 19 All-Ireland football medals with Kerry between 1975 and '86. Other famous names include the Grace brothers of Tullaroan in Kilkenny – Dick, Jack and Pierce – who won 15 All-Ireland medals in hurling and football with Kilkenny and Dublin. The Landers brothers from Tralee – Bill, John Joe 'Purty' and Tim 'Roundy' – won twelve between them and became the first set of three brothers to win All-Ireland medals on the same day when they defeated Mayo in the 1932 final in Croke Park, with veteran Bill making an appearance as a sub. The Landers's haul is matched by their fellow countymen, the Ó Sé brothers from Ventry – Darragh, Tomás and Marc – who, following in the footsteps of their uncle Páidí's haul of eight All-Irelands, have already accumulated a dozen Celtic Crosses. After an injury picked up in the semi-final ruled Darragh out of Kerry's 2004 final victory over Mayo, the three Ó Sé brothers eventually won an All-Ireland final on the field together in 2006 and '07. The Rackards of Wexford is another family name etched into the annals of GAA folklore. Nicky, Bobby and Billy Rackard won seven All-Ireland hurling medals between them (their grand-uncle was a member of the Wexford four-in-a-row football team of 1915–18) and lined out together in the 1955 and '56 successes. Three Sheehy brothers from Tralee – Paudie, Niall and Seán Óg, who was captain – played together on the Kerry team that won the All-Ireland football title of 1962, and three Connolly brothers from Castlegar – John, Michael and captain Joe – lined out for the Galway hurlers when winning the All-Ireland of 1980.

The influence of families often spans generations in the GAA, but pride of place goes to the Donnellan clan from Dunmore in Galway, which boasts three generations of All-Ireland winners. Mick Donnellan won an All-Ireland senior football medal with Galway in 1925, although in unusual circumstances. No All-Ireland final was actually played that year as Cavan and Kerry had been declared illegal. Mayo were nominated to represent Connacht and went on to defeat Wexford. However, they lost the subsequent Connacht final to Galway, who were then declared All-Ireland champions. Mick's son John took up the reins, captaining Galway to victory in the 1964 All-Ireland, although in tragic circumstances as Mick passed away during the match and John wasn't to find out until after the game. John added another brace of medals as Galway completed a three-in-a-row in both '65 and '66. Mick's grandson and John's son Michael Donnellan exploded onto the All-Ireland stage in 1998 when Galway defeated Kildare, and he added another medal in 2001.

Dublin footballer Bernard Brogan, who won All-Irelands with his own brother Jim, boasts three sons – Alan, Bernard Jnr and Paul – who have all worn the blue jersey, while four sons of Kerry footballers from the 1970s and '80s – Tommy Walsh, David Moran, Aidan O'Shea and Tadhg Kennelly, respectively the sons of Seánie Walsh, Ogie Moran, Jack O'Shea and Tim Kennelly – are currently members of the county squad.

Other famous GAA families include the Cork hurling dynasties of the Coughlans and the Ahearnes, who achieved huge success in the 1920s and '30s; the Mahers from Tubberadora – Jack and Mikey, and their nephews Sonny and Michael – collected fifteen All-Ireland medals between them; and the Fennellys of Ballyhale in Kilkenny, seven of whom played on the All-Ireland-winning club hurling side in 1981, a record matched in 1991 in football by the seven McGurk brothers from Lavey in Derry, though only five played in the final. In the 1980 club hurling final, five Connolly brothers lined out for Castlegar against six Donnelly brothers for Ballycastle. Then, of course, you have the seven Fennelly brothers from Ballyshale Shamrocks, three of whom – Ger, Liam and Kevin – won All-Irelands with Kilkenny, though not on the same day.

– HOLD ON A MINUTE –

Gaelic Games have something of a reputation for delaying competitions, but a special seven-a-side game organised in Naas, Co. Kildare, in 1924 stands apart from the rest. The match, between Naas and Caragh, was organised in conjunction with a carnival in the town, and after it finished in a draw, the medals were never presented and remained in the carnival secretary's drawer until he noticed that the game had never been replayed. The game was eventually replayed – in 1959, 35 years after the original fixture. This time, the teams were made up of sons of the men who had played in the original match.

– GAELIC SUNDAY –

On 4 August 1918, the GAA staged the biggest programme of fixtures in its history on a day that became known as 'Gaelic Sunday'. On the orders of the Central Council, more than a thousand matches were to be played throughout the country, an act of defiance against a ruling from the authorities of the time that permits would have to be obtained for all GAA-associated fixtures. An exact figure on the number of matches that actually took place that day is unknown, but it is thought that close to 2,000 hurling and football games were staged without major incident, and there was no display of police or military presence at any of the games the length and breadth of Ireland.

The Dublin County Board staged the biggest fixture of the day, the county intermediate football final in Croke Park, where over 1,000 gathered to take in the proceedings, which started just after 4 p.m. There was a small number of police officers at the entrance to the ground on Jones's Road, and they were called into action not to quell the threat of any riots or to halt the match, but to arrest unlicensed flag-sellers.

A total of 14 boys aged 12 to 17 years old were detained for hawking their wares outside the ground. To add to the festivities, a fife-and-drum band marched from the Dublin docks down Townsend Street and towards the city centre, gathering a sizeable crowd as they went. Some 500 people trailed the marching musicians by the time they got to O'Connell Bridge, but the congregation was too much for the local sergeant, who sent them all packing before they reached their destination at Croke Park.

Dublin County Board Secretary, Mr J.A. O'Toole, abiding by Central Council's request not to seek a permit from Dublin Castle, also staged matches at Ringsend Park, Sandymount, Clondalkin, Baldoyle, Crumlin, Clonsilla, Blackrock and Terenure.

– STAMP OF APPROVAL –

Images of great GAA players adorn the walls of GAA clubs and pubs the length and breadth of the nation, particularly after the All-Stars scheme was introduced in 1971. The presence of framed pictures of the recipients down through the years is often a sign that you're drinking in a 'GAA' establishment anywhere in the four corners of Ireland.

In 1999, the GAA and An Post collaborated to honour those selected on their Teams of the Millennium by having their faces stuck onto the top right-hand corner of envelopes around the country as they launched a set of postage stamps featuring pictures of the players.

The football team range was launched before the turn of the millennium, with Dan O'Keeffe, Enda Colleran, Joe Koehane, Seán Flanagan, Seán Murphy, J.J. O'Reilly, Martin O'Connell, Mick O'Connell, Seán O'Neill, Seán Purcell, Pat Spillane, Mikey Sheehy, Tom Langan and Kevin Heffernan joining the likes of Jesse Owens, Nelson Mandela and Mother Teresa in immortality by featuring on Irish postage stamps that year.

A year later, the hurling stamps were launched, with Tony Reddan, John Doyle, Nick O'Donnell, Bobby Rackard, Paddy Phelan, Brian Whelahan, Jack Lynch, Lory Meagher, Christy Ring, Mick Mackey, Jim Langton, Eddie Keher, Ray Cummins and Jimmy Doyle appearing alongside such luminaries as Albert Einstein, Pope John Paul II and Ludwig van Beethoven in the stamp book.

The trend continued in 2001 with the launch of the 'GAA Hall of Fame' series, featuring four players – two from each code – who were not selected on either millennium XV. Hurlers Nicky Rackard (Wexford) and Frank Cummins (Kilkenny) and footballers Jack O'Shea (Kerry) and Padraic Carney (Mayo) appeared on the commemorative stamps that year, and in 2002, the programme continued. Peter McDermott (Meath), Jimmy Smyth (Clare), Seánie Duggan (Galway) and Matt Connor (Offaly) were the four players chosen for the 'GAA Hall of Fame' series part two.

– CELEBRITY GAA FANS –

Dublin	Bertie Ahern, Bernard Dunne, Colm Meaney, Paul McGinley, Pádraig Harrington
Cork	Des Bishop
Limerick	J.P. McManus
Antrim	Gerry Adams
Tipperary	Niall Quinn
Offaly	Brian Cowen
Tyrone	Paul Brady
Meath	Hector Ó hEochagáin
Wexford	Jim Bolger

– GRAND SLAM GAA –

Irish rugby's three-year stint using Croke Park as its home while the redevelopment of Lansdowne Road was completed gave elite Irish sportspeople of a different code the chance to play in Ireland's greatest stadium. It also coincided with Irish rugby's most successful period in modern times, with the team winning six of the nine games (seven RBS Six Nations games and two autumn Tests) played there between 2007 and 2009. The only teams to beat Ireland in Croke Park were France's Grand Slam side of 2007, Wales's successful slammers of 2008 and the All Blacks in October of the same year.

But there are undeniably strong GAA roots within Ireland's 2009 Grand Slam-winning team. Tomás O'Leary knew all about playing in Croke Park, captaining the Cork minor hurlers to an All-Ireland title in 2001. O'Leary, of course, is son of the great Seánie O'Leary, one of the Rebels' three-in-a-row heroes of 1976 to '78, and winner of another in the centenary year.

Ireland full-back Rob Kearney missed a golden opportunity to play on the Jones's Road pitch well before he ever made his Ireland rugby debut. Kearney, who played his club football with Cooley Kickhams, was on the Louth minor squad for three years, and in his final season, 2003, the Wee County drew with Dublin in the Leinster semi-final. Kearney played midfield that day, as he did in the replay, when the Dubs went on to win by two points, clinching a Leinster final spot and the chance to play in Croke Park. He also appeared for Cooley Kickhams in a senior county final against neighbouring rivals St Mary's in 2004. Kearney's partner in the back three, Tommy Bowe, is another Grand Slam hero with a deep affinity with football. The Emyvale GFC clubman played on both the Monaghan under-16 and under-17 teams, but, contrary to widespread reports, never actually played as a minor for the county.

– FIFTEEN MINUTES OF FAME –

The iconic American artist Andy Warhol wasn't born until 17 years after the 1911 Leinster football final, but the concept of short-lived fame was certainly developed by the Meath team that year, who wore the provincial crown for less than half an hour. At 1.45 p.m. on 22 October, Meath were awarded the Leinster title because of a no-show by their opponents, Kilkenny. However, when the tardy Cats arrived 20 minutes later, the title was duly removed from the Royals and the game was played. Rather sickeningly for Meath, Kilkenny went on to win 2–4 to 1–1: the county's fourth and last Leinster football title.

– HOOP DREAMS –

As an official 'non-contact' sport, you wouldn't imagine that basketball players would make good footballers or vice versa, but there have been several exceptional examples in the recent past. Most notably, Kerry 'Star' Kieran Donaghy was plucked from the hardwood and Tralee Tigers' plans right into Jack O'Connor's Kerry full-forward line with explosive success.

Donaghy was, and is, recognised as one of Irish basketball's most talented players, and he had already won a National Cup and SuperLeague with Tralee in 2005 before his dramatic football intervention. Along with fellow Kerry panellist Mícheál Quirke, Donaghy went on to claim a second SuperLeague title with Tralee in 2008, scoring 21 points in their 66–62 victory over DART Killester – a tally that made him the game's top scorer.

As a teenager, Donaghy turned down a host of scholarships from America, unlike Mayo midfielder Ronan McGarrity. McGarrity won an Irish under-19 B Cup and was an Irish under-19 international before going stateside for four years on a basketball scholarship, and it was there, while playing football with New York, that he was first spotted as a potential Mayo star of the future. Like Donaghy and Quirke, McGarrity still plays SuperLeague basketball with his club, Merry Monk Ballina – whom he led to promotion in 2004 – whenever it doesn't coincide with football.

However, the only prominent intercounty footballer to play senior international basketball for Ireland was McGarrity's Ballina teammate Liam McHale, while former Dublin panellist Karl Donnelly also played basketball for his country.

Ireland did once have an international under-19 team featuring two future intercounty footballers, though. Longford's Trevor Smullen and Jason Sherlock both lined out in green together long before they caught the eye in their county colours. Despite being just 5 ft 9 in., Sherlock was one of the most prominent young hoopsters around and always stated the example of Muggsy Bogues (the Charlotte Hornets' 5 ft 3 in. point guard) as proof that when it comes to basketball, size doesn't matter.

– THE LONG COUNT –

In wider sporting circles, 'The Long Count' refers to the World Heavyweight boxing rematch between Gene Tunney and Jack Dempsey on 22 September 1927 in Soldier Field, Chicago. However, Meath GAA lore possesses its own version and one that is often relayed gleefully within the Royal County. The match was the Leinster quarter-final with Wicklow in 1954 and the Garden County were on the way to a famous victory, leading by three points at the end of the regulated sixty minutes. Yet they were still playing almost ten minutes later. As the shouts and bawls from the sidelines for the referee to blow the game up reached a crescendo and Wicklow players glanced curiously at the official, Paddy Meegan popped up to score the winning point, nine minutes over the allotted time! No rational explanation for the provision of such a lengthy added period was suggested other than the possibility that the referee's watch had broken and he was simply guessing the length of the half. Bill Delany of Laois was the referee of that game. Meath went forward and captured the All-Ireland that September.

– THE CRUCIATE –

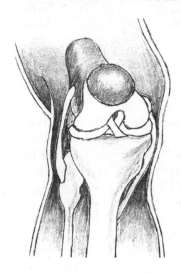

Cruciate knee-ligament injuries were probably unheard of in Gaelic Games until Kerry football legend and loquacious commentator Pat Spillane famously tore his in 1981, even though his fellow television pundit, former Meath star Colm O'Rourke, had suffered the same injury five years earlier. However, within a couple of decades the cruciate had become a common topic of conversation among GAA aficionados, particularly so given the frequency of this particular injury nowadays.

Besides Spillane, some of the other GAA stars of the past 30 years who have suffered the dreaded cruciate knee injury include Galway hurler Pete Finnerty, Kilkenny hurler Henry Shefflin, Tipperary hurler John Leahy, Galway footballer Seán Óg de Paor, Armagh footballer Kieran McGeeney, Dublin footballer Dessie Farrell, Meath footballer Trevor Giles, Cork footballer Graham Canty and Laois footballer Joe Higgins. The latter's injury became something of a cause célèbre as he subsequently received a ligament transplant from a dead American.

There are actually two cruciate ligaments in the knee – the posterior and the anterior – and they overlap in the middle to hold the knee in place and stop it sliding forwards or backwards. Medial and lateral ligaments perform the same function on either side of the knee. Cruciate injuries tend to occur when the knee is twisted or from blows to the side of the knee. While it is common to undergo surgery for this injury, it is not always compulsory, and treatment is usually preceded by a lengthy period of rehabilitation in which players build up the surrounding muscles to protect the knee. Dublin footballer Bobby Doyle was the first player to be officially declared a victim of the ailment.

– TWO-WEEK WONDERS –

In the early years of the twentieth century, it wasn't unusual for the All-Ireland finals to be delayed for up to two years. This staggered process led to Kilkenny, in 1905, enjoying the shortest reign as All-Ireland champions. The final was eventually played in Tipperary on 14 April 1907. The Cats took to the field in different-coloured jerseys while Cork togged out in an all-blue kit. Kilkenny, represented by the Erin's Own club, were facing St Finbarr's of Cork in a repeat of the 1904 decider, which was completed in 1906. Cork won the game 5–10 to 3–13, but Kilkenny objected on the grounds that the Cork goalkeeper Daniel McCarthy was a British Army Reservist. Cork counter-objected, arguing that a Kilkenny player had lined out with Waterford in the Munster Championship. The GAA's Central Council ordered a replay, which was held in Dungarvan on 30 June 1907 in front of a crowd of 10,000. Kilkenny's Jim Kelly ran amok, scoring 5–2 to give his side a 7–7 to 2–9 victory. However, their celebrations were short-lived. Two weeks later, they were defeated by Dublin in the Leinster final – the 1906 final, that is. Confused?

– PLAYERS' PLAYERS OF THE YEAR –

Unlike the GAA's All-Star awards, which are chosen by journalists, the Gaelic Players Association awards are selected from a shortlist by the players themselves. The awards were initiated by the players' body in 2001, and teams of the year were added in 2006.

GPA FOOTBALLER OF THE YEAR WINNERS

2001: Declan Meehan (Galway)

2002: Kieran McGeeney (Armagh)

2003: Steven McDonnell (Armagh)

2004: Matty Forde (Wexford)

2005: Stephen O'Neill (Tyrone)

2006: Kieran Donaghy (Kerry)

2007: Marc Ó Sé (Kerry)

2008: Seán Cavanagh (Tyrone)

GPA HURLER OF THE YEAR WINNERS

2001: Tommy Dunne (Tipperary)
2002: Henry Shefflin (Kilkenny)
2003: J.J. Delaney (Kilkenny)
2004: Seán Óg Ó hAilpín (Cork)
2005: John Gardiner (Cork)
2006: Henry Shefflin (Kilkenny)
2007: Dan Shanahan (Waterford)
2008: Eoin Larkin (Kilkenny)

GPA HURLING TEAMS OF THE YEAR

2006: 1. Donal Óg Cusack (Cork); 2. Eoin Murphy (Waterford); 3. Paul Curran (Tipperary); 4. Brian Murphy (Cork); 5. Tony Browne (Waterford); 6. Ronan Curran (Cork); 7. Tommy Walsh (Kilkenny); 8. Jerry O'Connor (Cork); 9. James 'Cha' Fitzpatrick (Kilkenny); 10. Dan Shanahan (Waterford); 11. Henry Shefflin (Kilkenny), 12. Martin Comerford (Kilkenny); 13. Ben O'Connor (Cork); 14. Eoin Kelly (Tipperary); 15. Joe Deane (Cork).

2007: 1. Damien Fitzhenry (Wexford); 2. Michael Kavanagh (Kilkenny); 3. Stephen Lucey (Limerick); 4. Jackie Tyrrell (Kilkenny); 5. Tommy Walsh (Kilkenny); 6. Ken McGrath (Waterford); 7. Mark Foley (Limerick); 8. James 'Cha' Fitzpatrick (Kilkenny); 9. Michael Walsh (Waterford); 10. Eddie Brennan (Kilkenny); 11. Ollie Moran (Limerick); 12. Dan Shanahan (Waterford); 13. Andrew O'Shaughnessy (Limerick); 14. Henry Shefflin (Kilkenny); 15. Martin Comerford (Kilkenny).

2008: 1. Brendan Cummins (Tipperary); 2. Michael Kavanagh (Kilkenny); 3. Noel Hickey (Kilkenny); 4. Jackie Tyrell (Kilkenny); 5. Tommy Walsh (Kilkenny); 6. Conor O'Mahony (Tipperary); 7. J.J. Delaney (Kilkenny); 8. Shane McGrath (Tipperary); 9. James 'Cha' Fitzpatrick (Kilkenny); 10. Ben O'Connor (Cork); 11. Henry Shefflin (Kilkenny); 12. Eoin Larkin (Kilkenny); 13. Eddie Brennan (Kilkenny); 14. Eoin Kelly (Waterford); 15. John Mullane (Waterford).

GPA FOOTBALL TEAMS OF THE YEAR

2006: 1. Stephen Cluxton (Dublin); 2. Marc Ó Sé (Kerry); 3. Barry Owens (Fermanagh); 4. Tom O'Sullivan (Kerry); 5. Seamus Moynihan (Kerry); 6. Bryan Cullen (Dublin); 7. Aidan O'Mahony (Kerry); 8. Nicholas Murphy (Cork); 9. Darragh Ó Sé (Kerry); 10. Alan Dillon (Mayo); 11. Alan Brogan (Dublin); 12. Ciaran McDonald (Mayo); 13. Conor Mortimer (Mayo); 14. Kieran Donaghy (Kerry); 15. Ronan Clarke (Armagh).

2007: 1. Stephen Cluxton (Dublin); 2. Marc Ó Sé (Kerry); 3. Darren Fay (Meath); 4. Conor Gormley (Tyrone); 5. Tomás Ó Sé (Kerry); 6. Aidan O'Mahony (Kerry); 7. Barry Cahill (Dublin); 8. Darragh Ó Sé (Kerry); 9. Nicholas Murphy (Cork); 10. Declan O'Sullivan (Kerry); 11. Alan Brogan (Dublin); 12. Paul Galvin (Kerry); 13. Colm Cooper (Kerry); 14. Paddy Bradley (Derry); 15. Tomás Freeman (Monaghan).

2008: 1. Anthony Masterson (Wexford); 2. John Keane (Westmeath); 3. Justin McMahon (Tyrone); 4. Conor Gormley (Tyrone); 5. Davy Harte (Tyrone); 6. Philip Jordan (Tyrone); 7. Ryan McMenamin (Tyrone); 8. Darragh Ó Sé (Kerry); 9. Enda McGinley (Tyrone); 10. Brian Dooher (Tyrone); 11. Declan O'Sullivan (Kerry); 12. Joe McMahon (Tyrone); 13. Colm Cooper (Kerry); 14. Seán Cavanagh (Tyrone); 15. Michael Meehan (Galway).

– MICK O'CONNELL – THE ISLANDER –

Mick O'Connell's birthplace on Valentia Island is something of a metaphor for his career – he was a footballer who was separated from the rest . . . athletic, strong, with a keen sense of team play and gifted in all the skills. Regarded as the most graceful practitioner of his sport, his reputation has endured – he remains a yardstick for midfielders in the most successful football county in Ireland.

The image of O'Connell gracefully rising to pluck a high dropping ball is one indelibly etched into the minds of a generation of Gaelic football fans, a portrait of athleticism and skill captured on the back of standard-issue Christian Brother jotter books for years after his retirement.

Born on 4 January 1937, O'Connell's father, Jeremiah, was a small farmer and fisherman who had left the now uninhabited island of Beginish. In isolation, with no football pedigree, the young Mick developed quickly into a prodigious talent, two-footed and consummate in the air.

He began his club football career with Young Islanders before making his mark as a Kerry minor in 1955. A year later, O'Connell made the step up to the Kerry seniors, and he won the first of his 12 Munster Championship medals in 1958, two fewer than the record set by Dan O'Keeffe in 1948. O'Connell's debut in Croke Park in the semi-final that year may have ended in a shock defeat to Derry, but O'Connell announced his arrival on the big stage after being moved into midfield to mark the great Jim McKeever.

After capturing the National League title in 1959, by which time O'Connell's high-fielding and elegant style had become his trademarks, he captained Kerry to success in the All-Ireland final against Galway, although he had to go off injured during the decider.

He picked up his second All-Ireland when Kerry defeated Roscommon in the 1962 final. However, over the next six years Kerry lost three finals, to Galway (twice) and Down, and it was 1969 before Kerry and O'Connell recaptured the Sam Maguire Cup. O'Connell won his fourth All-Ireland the following year as Kerry beat Meath. His last appearance in an All-Ireland final came in 1972 when Kerry lost to Offaly, and he retired the following year.

As well as four All-Irelands, O'Connell won six National League medals, twelve Munster Championship medals and an All-Star in 1972. He also played with Waterville, and won three county championship medals with the divisional side South Kerry.

In 1974, he published his frank and compelling autobiography *A Kerry Footballer*. Regarded as one of the greatest footballer of all time, O'Connell's background and the remarkable environment in which he had been brought up added to his mystique.

O'Connell, who later became an Independent county councillor, was named in midfield on the GAA's Football Team of the Century in 1984 and on the GAA's Football Team of the Millennium in 1999, which was commemorated on a postage stamp. He was inducted into the Kerry Hall of Fame in 2005.

– NICE BIT OF BUSINESS –

Croke Park is now known worldwide as the epicentre of the GAA, but it is a matter of fact that the purchase of the stadium in 1913 very nearly never happened. The background of the sale of the Jones's Road Sports Grounds, as it was then known, from GAA activist Frank Dineen, is widely known, but the GAA's Central Council was within a whisker of purchasing a ground on the other side of the Liffey. Motivated to buy a ground to call home and with relatively healthy financial resources, the GAA set up a committee consisting of members Luke O'Toole, Michael Crowe and J.J. Hogan to inspect venues around the capital. When they submitted their report to Central Council in 17 August 1913, it concluded that there were just two suitable options: the Jones's Road Sports Grounds, where they had been staging major events over the previous twenty years, and a fifteen-acre site at Elm Park in Dublin 4, owned by Lord De Frenche.

Dineen was willing to sell Jones's Road for £4,000, while the Elm Park ground was available for £5,000, but Dineen, sensing that Central Council were swaying towards the latter, dropped his price to £3,625. His suspicions proved correct, and at the next meeting on 14 September, the GAA power brokers proposed and seconded a motion to buy Elm Park. Before Central Council had time to act, Dineen further decreased his price to £3,500 – just £250 more than he paid for it – and eventually it was decided on a vote of eight to seven that the GAA buy the ground and name it after Archbishop Croke.

– EFFORTLESS –

Long-winded disciplinary sagas are one of the more tedious elements of the GAA, with players often hauled before the various committees to plead their case against suspension. Often, their defence is pinned on trying to convince the powers that be that a tackle was over-zealous rather than dangerous, but back in 1920, Kildare footballer Larry Stanley got slapped with a ban for entirely the opposite reason. Stanley was suspended for 'not trying hard enough' in a challenge game against Kerry, and he walked away from the game for a period in frustration at the charge. At the time, bookies hovered on the sidelines of most major matches, and the suspicion amongst the GAA hierarchy was that Stanley was in cahoots with the money-men. Kildare threatened to pull out of the 1920 Leinster Championship as a result, but eventually relented and played on without Stanley, who didn't return to his county colours until the 1926–27 season. He had already captained Kildare to victory in 1919, had been a member of the Dublin team that had won the All-Ireland of 1923, and played soccer for a while with Belfast Celtic.

– PLAY IT AGAIN, SAM –

A total of eight footballers have lifted Sam Maguire twice as All-Ireland-winning captains. By far the most successful of the elite bunch is Kerry's Joe Barrett, who won six All-Ireland medals over the course of his career. Tony Hanahoe also holds the distinction of being player–manager when he lifted the chalice for a second time as Dublin captain in 1977, while Enda Colleran could conceivably have been the only man to lead his county to three Sam Maguires, but the armband was handed to John Donnellan for the first of the Tribesmen's three-in-a-row years in 1964.

Joe Barrett (Kerry): 1929 and 1932

Jimmy Murray (Roscommon): 1943 and 1944

J.J. O'Reilly (Cavan): 1947 and 1948

Seán Flanagan (Mayo): 1950 and 1951

Enda Colleran (Galway): 1965 and 1966

Tony Hanahoe (Dublin): 1976 and 1977

Declan O'Sullivan (Kerry): 2006 and 2007

Brian Dooher (Tyrone): 2005 and 2008

– EVERYONE'S A WINNER –

When does a losing captain in a major final still get to hoist a trophy upon the conclusion of a game to the confused applause of his disappointed and bemused countymen? The answer is the National Hurling League final of the 1930–31 season. Uniquely for a league final, the clash between Tipperary and Galway preceded not one but two trophy presentations to the mildly bewildered masses. The big game was fixed for the newly built Castle Grounds in Portumna and, duly, the locals turned out in their droves. The

Tribesmen didn't let down the hefty home support, either, beating Tipp by a point, 4–5 to 4–4, and lifting the National Hurling League winners' trophy. However, there was one more presentation to make. The local parish priest decided that neither team should go away empty-handed for their exertions and purchased a second trophy, which he then presented to the losing Tipperary team.

– SINGING OUT OF TUNE –

The alteration of Rule 42 in the GAA's *Official Guide* and the opening of Croke Park to rugby and soccer may have provided a financial windfall for the GAA and paved the way for a deluge of goodwill from the Irish public, but it wasn't to the liking of everyone with the GAA. Former Kerry footballer, Wexford manager and respected writer J.J. Barrett took the decision to remove his father's All-Ireland medals from the GAA museum in protest against the singing of 'God Save the Queen' in Croke Park in 2007.

Barrett's father, Joe, won six All-Irelands in the 1920s and '30s, and later donated his Celtic Crosses to the GAA archive, but his son later wrote to then director general Liam Mulvihill to inform him of his reasons for taking back the medals. In his letter to Mulvihill, Barrett wrote:

> I believe that you as DG and the executive of the GAA also have a duty of care and a responsibility to all GAA members past and present to protect the ethos of the Association to which so many have contributed down the decades. The arrogant war-mongering words of 'God Save the Queen' ringing out over Croke Park is surely pushing the boundaries of tolerance and common sense beyond what is expected in any Republic on earth.

Barrett also said he would return the collection to Croke Park when the temporary arrangement between the GAA, the Irish Rugby Football Union and the Football Association of Ireland was over, hence terminating the possibility of the English national anthem being sung at the Jones's Road venue again. Barrett had initially proposed the English rugby team adopt a different anthem when playing in Croke Park, a suggestion rejected. For the record, 'God Save the Queen' was performed twice in Croke Park, for the 2007 and 2009 Six Nations clashes between Ireland and England.

– A REAL MAN'S GAME –

Gaelic footballers often pride themselves on the toughness of their chosen sport, particularly when the inevitable comparisons with soccer are raised. While patrons of Gaelic Games often tut tut at the theatrical antics and 'softness' of some soccer players, they revel in the hard-hitting, shoulder-to-shoulder clashes that are part of Gaelic football and hurling. One soccer player, however, who certainly could never have been accused of being 'soft' was Irish international Kevin Moran. The former Manchester United, Sporting Gijón and Blackburn defender developed a reputation as a no-nonsense stopper and one of the 'hard men' of that United team of the early '80s. He also has the dubious distinction of being the first player to be sent off in an FA Cup final, in 1985. Moran, of course, was steeped in Gaelic Games, and that upbringing is often cited by GAA people as the reason for his trademark toughness.

Moran won two All-Irelands with Dublin in 1976 and '77 and played in the 1978 decider, by which time he was already on Manchester United's books, and Dublin boss Kevin Heffernan had to make a request to United manager Dave Sexton for permission to play Moran in that year's All-Ireland final. Moran ended up in the wars in the days preceding the final and during the game itself. Heffernan took great delight in demonstrating to his opposite number at United just how physical the game of Gaelic football was. 'First of all, Kevin pulled a hamstring the Thursday before the final,' revealed Heffernan later. 'Then he had a collision during the match and had about six stitches across his forehead. We sent him back to Man United in bits with a note to tell them: "This is the way real men play."'

– STAY OFF THE GRASS –

Pitch invasions are still the norm at GAA grounds on the day of major finals despite the practice being eradicated in almost all other sporting codes across the world. They are also the source of much angst amongst GAA officials, who have tried, thus far in vain, to cease the practice of spectators encroaching onto the playing surface at the conclusion of games, although they are looking at the idea of seeking legislation to have the act outlawed. The 1956 Leinster football quarter-final was one such example of how a post-match invasion can mess up a championship royally for the Association. With at least five minutes remaining of the match, a spectator blew a whistle from amongst the thronging sideline mob, and duly, the considerable crowd rushed the pitch. Amid the ensuing confusion as officials tried to clear the field, someone made off with the match ball and the game had to be abandoned and replayed.

– TOUGH BREAK –

Hard luck stories are ten a penny in the GAA. From blind referees to short-sighted umpires and linesmen, there's no shortage of Gaels who have been done out of All-Ireland medals for one reason or another. Consider the case of Eddie Dowling, however. A Kerry footballer of great reputation, he was chosen to captain the Kingdom in 1946 as they bid to end a half-decade absence from the winners' podium in Croke Park. Dowling dutifully led his green-and-gold troops to Munster glory, but was controversially dropped for the All-Ireland final showdown with Roscommon. However, he came on as a substitute and turned the game around for Kerry, who had trailed for much of the match, and he was duly selected for the replay three weeks later. Dowling, though, must have wondered if he was cursed never to fulfil his destiny. In the build-up to the replay, Dowling broke his ankle and was forced to sit out Kerry's eventual dismissal of Roscommon, and with the Kingdom waiting a further seven years to reclaim Sam Maguire, Dowling never won an All-Ireland medal.

– DEAD SHERIFF –

They say you're only fully appreciated after you're gone, and that certainly was the case for Meath footballer Brendan Maguire. Maguire found himself in a strange bind back in 1952 when he lined out for the Royals against Cavan, for whom two of his brothers were playing. Perhaps the on-field family feud or the fact that Meath lost the final prompted Brendan's emigration, but he was to prove a big hit across the water, too. In 1986, he won an election for the post of sheriff in San Mateo County, polling 81,679 votes against the 20,839 for his nearest rival. Brendan never got to fulfil his role, however. Unbeknownst to the electorate, Maguire had died at the age of fifty-three some six weeks before the polls had opened.

– HURLING HEADGEAR –

Hurlers without helmets are a rarity nowadays, but the practice of using protective headgear only came into being in the 1970s and was initially slow to catch on. In fact, the first hurler to don a helmet during a match did so out of necessity rather than as a preventative measure. Mícheál Murphy, from the Blackrock club in Cork, is said to be the man that started the trend for donning a helmet after he suffered a fractured skull. Murphy initiated the new fad in the 1969 Fitzgibbon Cup final for UCC and continued wearing a helmet for the rest of his playing days. Donal Clifford of Cork was the first intercounty player to make helmets fashionable.

– DOUBLE-TAKE –

Here are a few GAA figures with famous namesakes.

- Eddie Rockett and Eddie Rocket (Waterford footballer and fast-food restaurateur)
- Darren Clarke (Louth footballer and Ryder Cup golfer)
- John Hayes (Cork footballer and Irish Rugby Football Union prop)
- Paul McGuigan (Monaghan footballer and former Oasis bassist)
- Michael Jordan (Wexford hurler and Chicago Bulls legend)
- Paddy Casey (former Offaly footballer and songwriter)
- Pat Kenny (Wexford hurler and former *Late Late Show* presenter)
- Mickey Harte (Tyrone football manager and Irish Eurovision entrant)

– STOUT DEFENCE –

Nowadays, the cost of running intercounty teams runs into millions for county boards, particularly those whose teams make it to the latter stages of their respective championships. But in 1942, the Dublin County Board was hit with an unexpectedly large bill for a social function being held to reward the county's successful All-Ireland-winning footballers. The hurlers, who reached that year's All-Ireland final, were also invited to the do, which took place in Clery's on O'Connell Street. The county board was due to foot the bill for the alcoholic refreshment.

At around 11.30 p.m., county board treasurer Tom Woulfe was approached by Beefy Kennedy, the one man to play in both All-Ireland finals that year, who informed Woulfe that the supply of drink had run out. Due to rationing, there was no whiskey available, so Guinness was the drink of choice for the night. Woulfe wrote an order for another 12 dozen bottles of stout and handed it to Kennedy to take to the storeman whose job it was to look after the needs of hotel's guests. County chairman Seán Ó Braonáin left at around 12.30 a.m., noting that the festivities had perked up and that the two panels of players were enjoying a more raucous night than he had expected.

That was the last he thought about it for another month, until an astronomical bill came through to the county board from Clery's. Kennedy, in his haste to maximise the generosity of the county board, had altered the order from 12 dozen stout to 72 dozen, and the party had gone on until four o'clock the next morning!

– STAR WARS –

The annual GAA All-Stars selections never fail to prompt controversy and debate over who should or shouldn't have made the team. Still, a couple of decisions have provoked the ire, fury and general bewilderment of the GAA masses and, in particular, those affiliated with the snubbed parties. In 1994, Brian Whelahan was awarded Texaco Hurler of the Year for his heroic displays with Offaly en route to their All-Ireland success, but despite being highly regarded as the best hurler in that year's championship, he wasn't deemed worthy of a place on the All-Star selection. The system of voting was blamed for the decision. Because the votes were taken as a secret ballot, Whelahan actually received more individual votes than any other half-back, but the votes were spread across the three half-back positions and he didn't receive the highest number of votes at either right half-back, centre-back or left half-back.

However, the furore over Whelahan was matched 11 years later by Tyrone legend Frank McGuigan. So disillusioned was Frank with the non-selection of his son Brian in 2005, he decided to auction off the award he himself won back in 1984. 'It's a farce,' fumed McGuigan, who went on to question the integrity of the selection committee, which is made up of GAA journalists. 'Football men like Colm O'Rourke should be in there,' he said.

He disputed the selection of Peter Canavan – despite his All-Ireland final heroics – and reckoned that not only was Brian's performance in the decider more worthy of an All-Star than his son's previous selection in 2003, it also surpassed Frank's own legendary Ulster final performance in 1984, when he kicked a total of 11 points from play against Armagh: 'Peter Canavan is Tyrone's best footballer ever, but Peter would be the first to say he was no All-Star this year. Brian deserved one this year more than he did when he won and more than I did in 1984. He mightn't have kicked 11 points, but he had a better game in the All-Ireland final than I had in that Ulster final.'

ARSE-BOXING –

Some words or phrases are either unique to the GAA or have had their meanings altered to fit in with the games. It's unlikely one will hear of anyone 'schkelping' another person outside the realms of a football or hurling match, while that often-used phrase 'a wide is as good as a score' would certainly draw curious glances were it not uttered in the dying throes of some GAA epic. Former Dublin boss Tommy Lyons went one further, though. Searching his vocabulary for a term to describe the hawking of merchandise to raise funds for team holidays, Lyons adopted and immortalised a word into the GAA lexicon: 'If you win an All-Ireland, you deserve two or three weeks away somewhere,' he said. 'Or whatever the group wants to do. And there should be no questions asked. What I don't like is this touting teams around, selling pictures of them and all that. I call it *arse-boxing*. That word is not in the dictionary, but it's a good enough word to describe it.'

– THE OTHER FELLA –

Maurice Davin is remembered as one of the founding members of the GAA, its first and the only two-time president, while his legacy was honoured by the Association in 2006 when the Canal End of Croke Park was renamed the Davin Stand. But Davin, a Tipperary native, was also part of a push to disband the GAA in 1889, and his exit from the Association was the cause of some controversy. Deep in debt over the non-payment of affiliation fees from clubs and the financially disastrous 1888 'Invasion' tour of America, the annual meeting of the GAA's top brass in 1889 erupted in recrimination over the fiscal predicament.

Davin was the focus for blame, and the meeting was thrown into disarray when the Limerick delegation left the meeting. Davin followed and met with the Limerick group, and between them, they devised a motion calling for Central Council to be disbanded and for county boards to run their own competitions from then on. However, Davin's exit was seen by the Central Council delegates still in the meeting as an act of resignation and, promptly, they voted Peter Kelly in as a new president. The Davin–Limerick motion was never heard, and the GAA's first president never again took any formal part in the Association until his death in 1927.

– FRUITFUL FAILURES –

The arrival of Joe Canning on the senior hurling scene was one of the most anticipated moments in recent GAA memory. The youngest of a family steeped in hurling, he had been asked into the Galway senior set-up as a 17 year old, but wisely elected to play out his three years at minor and a full year with the Galway under-21s before finally making the step up in 2008. Once his elevation was complete, though, the results were immediate and hugely impressive. Already built for top-level hurling, and with a striking technique that is comparable with the best in history, Canning set out to replicate his club and underage success with the Tribesmen's seniors.

In his first championship game, he hit 2–6 against Antrim. Canning's next trick was a nine-point haul against Laois, but it was the 'game of the season' in 2008 against Cork in the next round in which Canning earned a most unwanted honour. Against the Rebels, he hit 2–12 of their 2–15 total – the highest individual total of any player on a losing team in championship history. The previous holder of the unwanted distinction was Eddie Keher, who scored 2–11 for Kilkenny in the All-Ireland of 1971. However, that game was played over 80 minutes, making the young Portumna ace's achievement all the more remarkable.

But while Canning's elevation to senior status was long-awaited and eagerly anticipated, consider the case of Cork's Finbarr Delaney – another man high on the list of top-scoring losers. In 1989, Delaney made his championship debut at 33 years of age – some 15 years after playing in a successful Cork minor team. Delaney, an ace free-taker himself, scored a whopping 1–11 in the replayed Munster first-round clash with Waterford – and then never played for the Rebels again.

– IRISH WAYS AND IRISH LAWS –

The GAA views itself as a cultural organisation with a reach far beyond its ostensible role as a sporting body. The Association's *Official Guide* states that GAA members see it as a means of 'consolidating our Irish identity'. Arguably, the greatest cultural significance of the GAA really lies in its games, but the stated aims of the Association are much broader, for example, 'the strengthening of the National Identity in a 32 County Ireland through the preservation and promotion of Gaelic Games and pastimes'.

The additional aims of the GAA (which include the support of ladies' football and camogie, as well as the promotion of music and dance through the 'Scór' competitions) detail that the organisation should 'actively support the Irish language'.

The GAA's practical relationship with the Irish language is strongest in the western Gaeltacht regions of the country, where Gaelic is still actively spoken on a daily basis. There are a number of famous clubs situated in these regions, such as An Ghaeltacht in West Kerry; Mícheál Breathnach and An Cheathrú Rua in Connemara; and Naomh Columba, Naomh Abán, An Rinn and Gaoth Dobhair in Donegal. Every summer, a specific football tournament called Comórtas Peile na Gaeltachta is held for the Irish-speaking clubs. The event, held in a different Gaeltacht area every year, is an annual celebration of football and language, but it is also a competition taken very seriously by the senior and junior clubs involved.

A number of famous native-speaking players have graced the national stage, such as Galway hurlers Joe Connolly and his brothers John and Michael; Galway footballers Seán Óg de Paor and Seán Ó Dómhnaill; John Joe Doherty of Donegal; Kerry footballers Mícheál Ó Sé and Páidí Ó Sé, as well as Páidí's nephews Darragh, Tomás and Marc Ó Sé, along with fellow clubman Dara Ó Cinnéide; and Cork footballers Anthony Lynch and Mícheál Ó Cróinín. Furthermore, Cork hurling icon Seán Óg Ó hAilpín was raised speaking Irish despite being born in Fiji and growing up in Cork city. Former Galway captain Seán Óg de Paor actually penned his autobiography in Irish, while Ó Cinnéide works as an Irish-language broadcaster with Raidió na Gaeltachta. Nowadays, there are increasing numbers of Irish-speakers in all counties.

Joe Connolly delivered a famous acceptance speech entirely in Irish from the Hogan Stand after captaining Galway hurlers to All-Ireland glory in 1980, and Páidí Ó Sé, Ó Cinnéide and Ó hAilpín followed suit in 1985, 2004 and 2005 respectively. It is also GAA policy that all commentary on minor matches be in Irish.

Irish is used formally in general GAA administration, particularly in headings, greetings, titles and so on. It is also obligatory for official team sheets to be produced in the native language. While this may appear tokenistic, it could be countered that it is also positive reinforcement of the GAA's aims. Official GAA documents are produced bilingually. In recent years, the GAA has also produced handy promotional material to encourage the understanding of and use of Irish in general club activity. Irish-language classes are regularly held in GAA clubs, and every club and county board must appoint an Irish-language officer. It is also GAA policy that all commentary on minor matches be in Irish.

– LONELY PLANET GUIDE TO HURLING –

The Lonely Planet is one of the most widely used travel guidebook series in existence, providing a useful resource to millions of tourists all over the world. There are over five hundred publications in eight different languages, all of which give the casual traveller an in-depth feel for their destination of choice. Be it advice on places to stay, tips on what food to eat and where to eat it, guidelines on local culture, what to avoid or how to cope in the case of an emergency, the guides are researched by some of the top travel writers in the world, all of whom possess an intimate knowledge of the country or city about which they are writing.

And just like every other major European destination, Ireland was the subject of one of the Lonely Planet guides. The book contains all sorts of pointers about a quick trip to the country and naturally enough, there is an account of the writer's first encounter with hurling. Slightly whimsical it is too, as illustrated below:

> Hurling isn't what the Irish do when they've had too much Guinness (well, not always). It's actually a mad kind of aerial hockey invented to make the English feel embarrassed about tiggy-touchwood soccer. If you haven't had the twisted pleasure of seeing this example of man's inhumanity to man, head to the Emerald Isle but keep your head down. This 15-century-old activity pulls no punches. A hurling match is perhaps the fastest spectator sport in the world (with only ice hockey matching it for up-close frenzy). From a distance it resembles a roaming pack-fight between men with thin pale legs and names like Liam and Seán.
>
> At ground level it's much more frightening, a kind of 15-a-side escape from the asylum. Hurling is rapid, breakneck and rambunctious. The game moves too fast for the novice to understand anything but the most basic rules, but you can start by imagining an egg-and-spoon race with a pack of enormous angry stick-wielding roosters charging the leader.

– WALK-OFF –

Championship matches in the late part of the 1800s were pockmarked with walk-offs, objections and appeals, though one stands apart as slightly unique. A Leinster Senior Football Championship clash between Wexford and Kilkenny was halted prematurely when the Cats captain, Dick Kealy, complained of overly robust tackling from their opponents. At the time, they were 0–5 to 0–1 ahead, but had lost five of their players to the heavy hitting of the Kilkenny men. Expecting a boardroom walkover, Wexford prepared themselves for a provincial final only to be told that the match had been awarded to Kilkenny. They remain the only team to stage a walk-off in championship football while actually leading.

– THE HAMSTRING –

A hamstring injury is the most common type of muscle injury that causes hurlers and footballers to miss games, but older Gaels are fond of recalling a time when this injury apparently never occurred. However, such mythology is now ancient history as most players know all too well that horrible feeling when the back of the leg suddenly seems to 'snap' while chasing that elusive ball into the corner. Not all injuries are equally serious, of course; a hamstring strain usually occurs early in a match whereas a tear (in which there is actual fibre damage) is usually seen where muscle fatigue is a factor later in a match. The latter injury will lead to a slower recovery time. Time spent on the treatment table for a hurler or footballer can be reduced if the injury is treated properly in the initial stages, including ice and compression, early mobilisation and motion of the injured area and early massage of the affected muscle, all of which, of course, should be carried out with expert supervision.

– HEFFO –

Dublin legend Kevin Heffernan's achievements as a player and a manager may have been exceeded by his greatest rival, Mick O'Dwyer, in numerical terms, but Heffernan remains one of the most intriguingly appealing and elusive figures in Gaelic Games.

Credited not only with wrestling Dublin football out of the doldrums in 1974, Heffernan is also regarded as the man who modernised the image of Gaelic football throughout the 1970s by professionalising the preparation of his players in terms of fitness and tactics. This period was to have a profound effect on Gaelic Games in the capital in the sense that it finally provided an opportunity for them to rival the popularity of soccer and rugby. Huge crowds were drawn to watch Dublin, and that appeal has remained undiminished since. The commercial importance of the Dublin football team to the GAA in terms of attendances is a legacy of the Heffernan era. Ever since, the Dublin senior footballers have had the biggest following of any team of the code in Ireland.

Seemingly sated by the 1976 All-Ireland success over his nemesis Kerry, Heffernan was absent as Dublin overcame Kerry in the semi-final the following year, adding their third Sam Maguire Cup of the decade under player–manager Tony Hanahoe. However, Heffernan returned in 1978, only to witness his arch-enemies blossoming into the greatest Gaelic football team of all time under O'Dwyer.

Heavy defeats to the Kingdom in '78 and '79 could have ended Heffo's reign, but the Dublin man's ability to endure was unquestionable. He stayed on and constructed a new Dublin team around his greatest servant, Brian Mullins, guiding them to All Ireland success in 1983. The manager's implacable desire to prevail was evident as Dublin, reduced to 12 men in a fractious battle with Galway, overcame adversity.

Much of Heffernan's career as a player and manager was measured in terms of rivalry with Kerry. For thirteen successive years, between 1974 and 1986, either Dublin or Kerry contested the All-Ireland final, although Kerry remained the dominant partner, defeating Dublin on five occasions during that period. Dublin did, however, overcome Kerry twice: in 1976 and in the famous 1977 semi-final.

Heffernan was born in Dublin in 1929, and his family moved to the then recently constructed estate of Marino, just outside the north inner city. The St Vincent's GAA club was founded in Marino in 1931. A pupil of Scoil Mhuire Marino and St Joseph's CBS in Fairview, Heffernan was introduced to Gaelic Games in school and went on to win a Leinster colleges medal with Joey's.

A seriously talented dual star, he won a staggering fifteen senior county football medals with St Vincent's, including seven in a row from 1949 to 1955, and six county hurling medals. A dual minor player with the county, Heffernan graduated to the senior football ranks with Dublin while still in his final year in school, and broke his jaw in a match just days before sitting his first Leaving Cert exam.

Two National League successes with Dublin in 1953 and 1955 were overshadowed by a three-point defeat to Kerry in the '55 All-Ireland final, where he lined out at full-forward. Three years later,

Heffo captained Dublin to a third National League success, and he lifted the Sam Maguire later that year when Dublin defeated Derry in the final. However, a year later Dublin lost narrowly in the semi-final to a Kerry team that included Mick O'Dwyer at wing-back. Heffernan rattled the woodwork four times as Dublin fell short. Dublin regained the title in 1963; however, by this time Heffernan had retired as a player.

He crossed paths with O'Dwyer again in the 1975 All-Ireland final when Kerry's young 'team of bachelors', as they were known (none of them was married), denied the champions, announcing a decade of intense rivalry between both managers and their respective counties.

After retiring from intercounty management, Heffernan went on to manage Ireland in the Compromise Rules victory over Australia in 1986. He was named at left corner-forward in the GAA's football Team of the Century and the Team of the Millennium. In 2004, aged 74, he managed St Vincents' under-15 hurlers to victory in the Dublin Championship. He was granted the Freedom of the City of Dublin in 2005.

Though he has always shunned the media spotlight, Heffernan's influence on the Dublin GAA scene has remained undiminished since his retirement, and his presence is felt to this day.

– QUALIFIED SUCCESS –

The recent annual debate over whether winning one's provincial title is ultimately more beneficial to a team than a backdoor assault on the All-Ireland remains inconclusive. In the eight All-Ireland football championships between 2001 and 2008, four provincial champions have gone on to lift Sam, while the same number of counties have discarded a beating in their own province and successfully negotiated a qualifier campaign to September success. In fact, of the sixteen All-Ireland finalists in that same time frame, eight had won early summer honours in Leinster, Ulster, Munster or Connacht, while eight had been jilted within their own province en route to the Sam Maguire decider. Galway were the immediate beneficiaries of the new system in 2001 when they recovered from a Connacht semi-final loss to Roscommon to win an All-Ireland title in the first year of the new championship format, while two of Tyrone's three All-Irelands between 2003 and 2008 have come off the back of provincial failure.

Increasingly, there is a feeling that actually winning provincial honours matters little in the bigger All-Ireland scheme. However, the contrasting cases of Kerry and Dublin are worth considering in this regard. Between 2001 and 2008, both counties won five provincial titles each. Kerry have gone on to appear in no fewer than six All-Ireland finals, winning three, while Dublin have failed in every year to even reach football's September showcase.

In hurling, the body of evidence supports provincial winners. Between 1997 – the inception of the backdoor system – and 2008, ten of the twelve All-Ireland hurling champions have first won their provincial championships, with Offaly (1998) and Cork (2004) the only teams to defy convention and lift the Liam MacCarthy Cup after losing earlier in the summer.

– STICK TO THE GOLF –

Pádraig Harrington's trophy-laden career as a professional golfer will be the source of much pleasure for Irish sports fans long after he has retired and putted the final ball of his heroic stint at the top of his sport. The multi-Major winner will be remembered as one of Ireland's greatest sportspeople of all time. But did you know he played in Croke Park? It was for his school, of course, and with all the success on the golf course, his tale of playing in GAA headquarters might just not make his autobiography. While he now spends his time chasing Tiger Woods down the fairways, he does recall, fondly, chasing a plucky young forward from St Vincent's School up and down the pitch.

'I was 16 and playing for Coláiste Éanna in the schools finals in Croke Park,' tells Harrington. 'I was normally full-back. A little bit stout then, not the fitness person I am now. We'd done our homework and reckoned the St Vincent's centre-forward was their best player. I have to say, when he walked onto the pitch, I didn't think he looked that much. Then the ball was thrown in and knocked down from midfield to him. And you'd want to see him go. It was a wet pitch, and he had me turned in an instant. I went to go after him and slipped, and to this day I still have treatment on my left wrist, I sprained it so badly. And that was my last game of football. I played on for the match, but, wow, he was quick. And it's very hard to tackle someone who dribbles the ball six inches off the ground.'

And who was the elusive young forward who had run rings around the future British Open champion?

'Dessie Farrell,' quipped Harrington. 'He ended my career!'

– EARNING YOUR STRIPES –

In the early days of intercounty competition, most sides wore the jerseys of their county champions, but between the mid-1910s and the late 1920s, that all changed as teams nailed their colours to the mast, so to speak. However, such was the eagerness of both clubs and counties to adopt the colours of the national flag, Leinster held a special competition to decide which of the 12 counties of the province would get the sole right to adorn the same image as the tricolour. Offaly duly won and have proudly donned the green, white and orange ever since.

– THE KEADY AFFAIR –

The practice of top intercounty players making cross-Atlantic trips to play for American football and hurling teams in their local championships was, until recently, one of the few real financial perks for elite GAA players. In the mid to late 1990s, such was the influx of famous faces from Ireland to play one or two games in places like Boston, Chicago and New York that they were given the nickname 'Aer Lingus All-Stars' by disgruntled locals – many of whom were irked at losing their places in their teams to the blow-ins. However, not everyone who was invited to play enjoyed the experience. Galway hurler Tony Keady made one such trip in 1989, after receiving assurance that it was within GAA law for him to do so, and played a challenge game for a local side in New York.

At the time, Keady was Texaco Hurler of the Year for his performances in Galway's 1988 Liam MacCarthy Cup triumph, and had played another key role in their National League success the following year. However, weeks after his return from New York, the GAA's Games Administration Committee informed the Galway County Board that Keady's appearance in the States was, in fact, against the rules and that he had played illegally. Keady was banned for a year, causing uproar amongst the Tribesmen and putting an enormous dent in Galway's three-in-a-row ambitions. For a while, Galway even contemplated pulling out of the championship, but they soldiered on without their star in the end. In the All-Ireland semi-final, Galway were beaten by Tipperary for the first time since 1971 after having two players sent off in an ill-tempered match.

The 'Keady Affair', as it became known, served to warn Tipp as well. They dropped Paul Delaney from their team for the game after it transpired that he had played in the London Championship without proper clearance.

– CLAMPED –

In 2005, when the Ulster final was moved from its regular venue of Clones to Croke Park to accommodate supporters hoping to see Armagh and Tyrone do battle in the provincial decider, the occasion sparked off-field controversy. No, there were no tunnel melees or riots in the stands, but a menace of a different description: clampers. According to reports, Dublin City Council clamped roughly 100 cars, all in the close vicinity of Croke Park. The mass crackdown on illegal parking on a Sunday in North Dublin sparked a wave of criticism for the council, which was accused of deliberately targeting cars with northern registrations. In fact, it prompted GAA director general Liam Mulvihill to lash out at the clampers, who, he claimed, had immobilised cars that were parked legitimately: 'Our members from Armagh and Tyrone were incensed last year by the number of cars clamped during games, which was way in excess of the numbers clamped on other occasions, which often at times appear to be legally parked,' he wrote in his annual report. Mulvihill then criticised the authorities for their lack of explanation: 'It is extraordinary that the Dublin Chamber of Commerce and the City Council, which purport to have the healthy vibrancy of the city at heart, are both silent when events in Croke Park are targeted.'

Eventually, the powers that be issued a statement denying the allegation that they had targeted cars with northern registrations and rejected the accusation that the vehicles were not in breach of parking laws. 'Clampers operate in conjunction with Gardaí and they clamp cars which are illegally parked,' said a spokesperson.

However, in the years since the outcry, there has been no further controversy whenever Ulster teams – or any other county for that matter – play in Croke Park, meaning either the clampers have taken to the spirit of the Gael or GAA supporters have learned where to park their cars!

– FAITHFUL HERO –

Offaly hurler Brian Whelahan might have been at the centre of two of the oddest All-Star selection controversies in the history of the scheme, but his position in the pantheon of hurling greats is undisputed.

And in a dazzling career that yielded two All-Irelands, the high point came in 1998 when Whelahan won his third All-Star after another incredible year for the Faithful that saw them come through the backdoor system, lose an All-Ireland semi-final that was blown up early, but win the replayed fixture and then beat Kilkenny in the final.

In that decider, Whelahan, who was suffering from flu in the build-up to the game, was moved from his regular wing-back berth to full-forward after just 16 minutes and scored 1–6 en route to his second Celtic Cross.

Whelahan, despite playing all previous seven matches in defence, was given the All-Star that year at full-forward. He did, however, inherit the distinction of being the first hurler to win All-Stars both as a defender and as an attacker, while further recognition was to come his way when he became the only active player to be named on the GAA's hurling Team of the Millennium. He also played a pivotal role in his club Birr's remarkable four All-Ireland, seven Leinster and twelve Offaly Championship successes.

– DUAL ALL-STARS –

Just four players have won All-Star awards in both football and hurling, and only one has managed it in the same year. Cork's Ray Cummins collected a pair of All-Stars in 1971, and with the gradual extinction of the intercounty dual player, it looks unlikely that that record will be broken. Two of Cummins's fellow Rebels have won All-Stars in both football and hurling, though neither Jimmy Barry-Murphy nor Brian Murphy can boast Cummins's achievement of collecting the awards in the same season. Liam Currams of Offaly is the fourth player to win the individual award in both codes.

– SPOT THE ODD ONE OUT –

Of the fifteen men to start the 1938 All-Ireland hurling final for Dublin (their last Liam MacCarthy success), Jim Byrne was the odd one out. The reason? Jim was from Dublin. All 14 of his teammates who beat Waterford that day were country-born but hurled with clubs in the capital. Byrne, an Eoghan Ruadh club man, was the only player born, bred and reared in Dublin and was considered the only real 'Dub' to have won an All-Ireland hurling medal. The situation forced Eoghan Ruadh to act, and in 1947, they submitted a motion to the county board that all Dublin teams be confined to native-born players and non-natives who had played from minor level up. The motion was passed on a vote of seventeen to three, but the rule wasn't implemented until the early 1950s, when the success of the all-Dublin St Vincent's footballers prompted a change in policy over capital representation.

– SCORING GOALKEEPERS –

While there has been a cluster of hurling goalkeepers who have managed to get themselves on the scoreboard in championship matches, football net-minders have had less luck troubling their opposing numbers in championship fare. One exception, though, was Roscommon's colourful custodian Shane Curran. Back in 2004, in Markiewicz Park, Roscommon and Sligo met in their Connacht semi-final replay and Curran managed to score not once, but twice! First, he converted a penalty in the forty-fourth minute – the third of the match – and then a 40-m free from the sideline sailed over the bar to give what looked like a game-winning advantage to Roscommon before Sligo's Johnny Davey forced extra time. Roscommon won in added time, though, with Curran finishing as Roscommon's joint top scorer along with Ger Heneghan.

In fact, Curran had been at the centre of a massive controversy in 1989, some 15 years previously, due to his penchant for placed balls. In that year's Connacht minor final, the Rossies faced a much fancied Galway side in Castlebar. Two points down in injury time, Roscommon were awarded a penalty, and as their designated kicker lined up to take the pressure kick, Curran emerged from nowhere to blast the ball to the net. Cue boisterous celebration from the Roscommon camp and an outbreak of outrage from the Tribesmen. Despite Roscommon being awarded the cup, Connacht

Council ordered a replay due to Curran's misdemeanour, but they went on and won that game too.

OTHER SCORING FEATS BY HURLING GOALKEEPERS

1982: Legendary Kilkenny hurling keeper Noel Skehan scores a point from an enormous distance in the All-Ireland semi-final against Galway.

1986: Galway net-minder John Commins becomes the only goalkeeper to score a goal in an All-Ireland hurling final when he buries a penalty against Cork in Croke Park.

1995: Clare keeper Davy Fitzgerald sprints up the pitch to take a penalty in the Munster Senior Hurling Championship final against Tipperary. He dispatches the shot with typical venom and performs a now-famous leap in the air as he darts back to his goal.

2007: Wexford goalkeeper Damien Fitzhenry blasts a late penalty past his opposite number to secure victory over Tipperary in the All-Ireland Senior Hurling Championship quarter-final.

– NO DRINK FROM THE CUP –

The GAA's tangled relationship with the demon drink drew top-level attention in 2008 when a motion from Laois was passed at Congress that forbade the filling of all Association trophies with drinks containing alcohol. Given the uncountable number of trophies in circulation around the country, a sceptical question was raised from the floor as to how exactly the new drink ban would be policed. Nickey Brennan, GAA president at the time, had a very practical and effective way of making sure alcohol would no longer be swilled from cups. 'There's nothing wrong with taking a small drill and boring a hole in the cup,' he suggested. As yet, we've yet to hear whether Sam Maguire and Liam MacCarthy have sprung deliberate leaks, but the Kerry County Board quickly gave its backing to the idea. Brian Sugrue, the Alcohol and Substance Abuse Prevention Officer in the Kingdom, went on to table a motion at county board level that trophy presentations not take place in clubhouse bars.

– FOUR-IN-A-ROW –

Wexford isn't short of notable GAA families. The Jacobs, the Dorans, the Rackards: famous football or hurling kin are part of the successful fabric of Gaelic Games in the county. However, one other Wexford family holds a national distinction that has yet to be broken. The Quigley brothers, John, Martin, Dan and Pat, are the only set of four from the same family to score in Senior Intercounty Championship hurling.

– GLASNOST –

While Gaelic Games at both club and intercounty level are now exposed to an enormous raft of publicity through the media, things were slightly different in the 1950s and '60s, when the GAA kept a close eye on what was written and said about the Association. Take Seán Óg Ó Ceallacháin, for instance. One of the longest-serving broadcasters in the world, he felt the full force of the GAA propaganda machine back in 1955 when he presented RTÉ's Sunday GAA programme. At the time, the GAA had a sort of editorial control over the coverage of the national broadcaster. But Ó Ceallacháin himself once fielded a phone call from the GAA's general secretary at the time, Pádraig Ó Caoimh, to demand that he cease to name players who had been sent off during matches. After Ó Ceallacháin objected, Ó Caoimh informed Seán that he could always be replaced. Luckily for the ideal of free speech, Ó Ceallacháin continued to inform the public which players had got the line, and given his longevity as a broadcaster, it's probably fair to say his career wasn't hindered too much.

– CARTOON CAMÁNS –

Everybody knows the importance of sport in the physical development of children, but more recently hurling has been used by animators as a sort of educational tool in the RTÉ cartoon *Ballybraddan*. The series aired in April 2009 and follows the lives of the fifth-class children of a local primary school. The series demonstrates how each child overcomes different obstacles in their growth into teenagers through the medium of hurling.
The show's producers described it as:

One place where they can really show what they're made of. One place where they learn to work as a group, a team . . . *Ballybraddan* follows the lives of these children and the adults that support them as they grow, mature, play, compete and find out who they really are. On and off the pitch, everyone needs to find their own place.

The programme followed swiftly on the launch of *C'mon Camán* in early 2009, a ten-part children's series also on RTÉ that saw budding young hurlers around the country showcasing their skills on the small screen for the first time.

Another RTÉ production, *Celebrity Bainisteoir*, saw a host of famous Irish personalities take the reins at junior football clubs around the country in a tournament designed specifically for the programme, which drew massive ratings for the broadcaster in its maiden year in 2008. Marty Whelan's Maryland team won the inaugural tournament, beating Gerald Kean's Mayfield side in the final. The series has featured such notable managers as Andrea Roche, Glenda Gilson and George Hook.

– TONGUE-TIED –

The influx of young footballers and hurlers from non-Irish backgrounds has been one of the most welcome developments in the GAA in recent years, and it has seen some more exotic-sounding names making it on to the referee's team sheets each week. There have been a couple of famous cases of GAA tongue-twisters in the past, however. Back in 1949, a man by the name of Paddy Ruschitzko, Polish by ancestry, captained the Laois hurlers to a Leinster title. Ruschitzko, or 'Rusty' as he was known, was born in New York but was brought up in Bagenalstown, and remains the last man to lead the O'Moore County to a provincial hurling crown and a place in the All-Ireland final. Perhaps an even more renowned hurler, though, is Lorenzo Ignatius Meagher, or 'Lory', as he became known. Meagher was Kilkenny born and bred, though the name 'Lorenzo' had been in the family for years.

– EVOLUTION OF THE FOOTBALL –

A modern Gaelic football is 25 cm in diameter and 69 to 74 cm in circumference. A dry ball weighs between 370 and 425 g, about 85 g heavier than a soccer ball. The panels on the ball are stitched horizontally and consist of six groups perpendicular to one another, each group being composed of two trapezoidal panels and one rectangular panel, 18 panels in all. Ireland's most famous sportswear manufacturer, O'Neill's, has been indelibly linked to the GAA since the company was established in 1918, and while no longer the exclusive supplier to the Association, it remains the dominant producer. O'Neill's is synonymous with Gaelic footballs in particular, with the brand logo a dominant feature of the ball.

1895: Standard-size 12-panel brown pigskin leather ball is introduced. Panels help ball to stay round.

1918: O'Neill's Sports Company founded.

1924: White ball first used in Croke Park because brown ball considered hard to see.

1932: White ball to be used in All-Ireland finals.

1968–9: Synthetic materials used and modern 18-panel Gaelic ball introduced.

– OLD SILVER –

The oldest trophy in Gaelic Games is the Sigerson Cup, which dates back to 1911 and pre-empts both the Sam Maguire and Liam MacCarthy Cups by a decade. The silverware was donated to the GAA by Dr George Sigerson, a poet from Strabane in Tyrone and a professor at UCD, and it heralded the beginning of the third-level football competition.

– FOOT-IN-MOUTH QUOTES –

'Being a Kerry manager is probably the hardest job in the world because Kerry people, I'd say, are the roughest type of f***ing animals you could ever deal with. And you can print that.'

> *– Former Kerry player and manager, Páidí Ó Sé in the* Sunday Independent *in January 2003*

'What I meant in the article about the Kerry supporters is that they are very hard to please, always demanding the highest standards, because they are a very proud race of people.'

> *– Páidí apologises to the Kerry people*

'If Galway don't win an All-Ireland in two years then I am a failure.'

> *– Prophetic words from Ger Loughnane on being appointed Galway manager in 2006*

'Tyrone have a lot of bad players. Brian Dooher is a bad player. I have a very expensive hat and I will eat it on this show if Tyrone win an All-Ireland and Brian Dooher is on the team.'

> *– TV pundit and former Meath footballer Colm O'Rourke in 2003 before Tyrone won their first of three All-Irelands*

'Hurling is the best field sport I have ever seen: it's much better than Gaelic football, which is really a mongrel of a game without a pedigree.'

> *– Soccer pundit Eamon Dunphy*

'I swear to God my mother would be faster than most of those three fellas, and she has a bit of arthritis in the knee.'

> *– TV pundit and former Kerry footballer Pat Spillane criticises the Armagh full-back line at half-time in the 2002 All-Ireland final between Armagh and Kerry*

'Death of hurling immortal.'

> *– Headline in the* Tipperary Star

'Speaking of Crossmaglen, I did a gig there one night and I asked, what was the big club there? Immediately, about 14 fellas shouted in unison: "Rangers." "Okay lads," I said, "all together now . . . It was old but it was beautiful . . ." I lasted five minutes.'

– *Comedian and former Down minor footballer Patrick Kielty prompting a singing of the Sash in the heart of South Armagh*

– EARLY PLAYER POWER –

The following is a letter from James Kelleher, Honorary Secretary of the Dungourney Hurling Club, on 11 August 1908:

Dear Sir,

I have been asked by your correspondent in the last issue of THE CORK SPORTSMAN to give my reasons for four picked men not travelling to do battle for Cork against Limerick on Sunday last week.

The principal objection in the way is the distance to Ennis. Imagine a man travelling 120 miles by rail to a match, which should be played thirty miles from the City of Cork. Starting from Dungourney at six o'clock in the morning, walking six miles to the railway station, going on to Cork, Mallow, Limerick, then into Co. Clare and playing a hard hour's game, starting from the latter place at half past six in the evening and arriving home at two or perhaps three o'clock next morning. We have done it before and will be prepared to do it again if we are required by any of the hurling teams in Cork. Give me the name of the County Board, Munster or General Council man who will do it? Would they walk half a mile from the station to the playing ground without a car while the players have to rely always on shanks' mare? I have seen, to my disgust, the players draw the crowds, make the money and lose their sweat at many a hard hour's game, while those gentlemen at the head of affairs take charge of the bag and jump in their cars again before the match is over – off to their hotel to count the coin made by the rank and file.

They will scoff at the application from injured players for compensation. We have several instances of it. At the last two finals – the All-Ireland one at Dungarvan and the Railway Shield at Kilkenny – where the gates totalled £440, six applications came before the meeting of the Central Council on 2 August, and the certificates sent in the usual way – five from Kilkenny men and one from a Dungourney man in Cork. The Dungourney certificate stated that this man was unable to work for five weeks. Alderman Nowlan, be it said to his credit, urged on the meeting the necessity to treat the men fairly and was ably supported by Mr Lalor, Kilkenny. In the face of this we find that the Cork representative – a gentleman by the name of Mr James Harrington – moved the reflection of all the applications, and in support of his motion said that none of the players left the field, whilst the other Cork representatives said nothing. After a lengthy discussion the six applicants were rewarded the handsome sum of £7. Who made all this money? Was it Mr Harrington might I ask? No. The men who risked life and limb are forgot, five of them £1 each, the other £2. If I am rightly informed, that man – put in that position by the Gaels of Cork – never caught a hurley in his hand, never felt the sting of the ash on his shinbones, does not know what it is to be laid up. When that man acts like this in the Central Council, what inducement is held out to players by the Munster Council when he is Chairman of that body?

When Mr Thomas Dooley represented Cork he always did his best towards injured players, but was cast aside at the last convention. Kilkenny have threatened their withdrawal from the Central Council. Dungourney can do the same and what is the case with Kilkenny and Dungourney today will be the case with the other counties tomorrow. It is time for the Gaels of Ireland to wake up, take the bags from these gentlemen, show them the outside of the gates and have men of the type of Austin Stack, Maurice McCarthy, Dick Fitzgerald and Dan Fraher at the head of the Association in Munster. The governing body has been captured by non-players, and the players themselves – the men who pay the freight – seem to have no direct representation on it. As Dungourney were champions for 1907, and this year is yet unfinished, I think they were entitled to as many representatives as any club in Cork.

The letter was written to the editor of the *Cork Sportsman* newspaper on 11 August 1908 and is an example of how tensions between administrators and players over money and expenses have existed since the formative days of the GAA. In an amateur organisation such as the GAA, power, not money, is its real currency. Players have often felt frustrated by their lack of power despite the fact that it is the money generated by players through intercounty gate receipts and, in recent years, sponsorship and broadcast rights, that has sustained the Association.

– OPEN FOR BUSINESS –

'I had people come to me from clubs saying that while they were opposed to opening Croke Park to soccer and rugby, they had people coming to them in their own clubs saying "if you vote 'no', then don't be coming to us and asking us to buy lottery tickets and raffle tickets."'

– Former GAA president Seán Kelly

Undoubtedly, the GAA's current rude financial health has benefited from the removal of Rule 42 and the rent that the Association receives for the use of the stadium by both the FAI and the IRFU. In the three years that Croke Park has been open to soccer and rugby, the stadium has staged a total of twenty-one 'foreign' games. For each of these occasions, the GAA receives a rent of €1.3m or 26.5 per cent of the ticket revenue – whichever is higher. That means that over the course of the period, the GAA has made a minimum of €27.3m out of the arrangement.

– CUSACK IN *ULYSSES* –

The parodying of GAA players, managers and broadcasters on television and radio is an amusing recent development, but perhaps the most famous example of a fictional character being based on a factual GAA figure is in James Joyce's epic *Ulysses*. The character 'The Citizen' in the Cyclops episode of the novel is thought to be at least partly based on one of the GAA founding fathers, Michael Cusack. Joyce wrote: 'The figure seated on a broad boulder at the foot of a round tower was that of a broadshouldered deepchested stronglimbed frankeyed redhaired freelyfreckled shaggybearded widemouthed largenosed longheaded deepvoiced barekneed brawnyhanded hairylegged ruddyfaced, sinewyarmed hero.' Beats normal, run-of-the-mill sports writing.

– THE INVASION –

Long before All-Star tours or the Polo Grounds final, the GAA took its best athletes across the Atlantic; and while the 'Invasion' of 1888 showcased Ireland's indigenous games and brightest sportspeople to a whole new audience, the chief reason for the trip was money.

The GAA's Central Council decided in 1888 to resume the ancient Tailteann Games, a festival of sporting competitions for all athletes of Irish extraction. The one hitch they hit, though, was a financial one. It was estimated that to host the games in Dublin, the GAA would require a £5,000 injection to their coffers. So to raise the funds, it was proposed that the GAA send 50 of its finest hurlers and athletes to America to stage sporting exhibitions and raise money stateside.

Unfortunately, even generating the initial cost of the trip proved troublesome and departure was delayed until September 1888. Upon arriving in New York, however, the party met a front of widespread apathy. Events were staged in New York, Philadelphia, Patterson, Newark and Boston, but with an American presidential election in progress and in a month of torrential rain, few bothered to attend. The trip succeeded in planting strong roots for the GAA on the American East Coast, but it was a disaster in terms of the intended purpose: generating cash. Instead of raising the £5,000, the group actually required a loan of £400 from Michael Davitt to fund the trip home, a journey that was made without a large portion of the group, many of whom stayed and settled in America and never again graced the GAA pitches of Ireland.

– BLESS ME, FATHER –

Constitutionally, the GAA is a non-sectarian organisation, but like most Irish institutions, it became entwined with the Catholic Church following the foundations of the Irish Free State in 1922. There have been a number of prominent Protestant members of the GAA, such as the Sam Maguire Cup's namesake and former president Jack Boothman, but partition and the separation of education in Ireland meant that the GAA was subject to the same religious divide as most other organisations. The direct link between the GAA club and the parish meant that priests played a prominent role in the development of the Association. This wasn't the case in the early years of the GAA, when the Catholic hierarchy was largely hostile towards the Association, seeing it as a haven for Fenians. Although the Archbishop of Cashel, Dr Thomas Croke, had been appointed as one of the GAA's first patrons, as a man who believed passionately in the revival of Gaelic Games he was something of an exception among the clergy in late nineteenth-century Ireland. Such was the strain between priests and the Fenians within the GAA that a fight actually broke out during the annual convention in 1887.

Tensions between the Church and the revolutionaries during the War of Independence were reflected in the GAA in general, but relations warmed considerably after 1922, and the sight of a leading church figure throwing in the ball on All-Ireland final day became a regular one up until the 1970s, when the influence of the Catholic Church in Ireland began to wane.

Playing priests were rare enough in the early twentieth century, although there were exceptions, such as Mundy Prendiville, who walked out of a Dublin seminary to play with Kerry in an All-Ireland final in 1924. As Ireland became more liberal, so the volume of priests playing the games grew to the point where men such as Offaly footballer Fr Nicholas Claffey and Galway hurler Fr Iggy Clarke became stars of the games in the 1970s and '80s. The latter indeed enjoyed quite a fearsome reputation as a hurler, and former Antrim star and subsequent manager Sambo McNaughton said of him, 'My innocent perception of the priesthood changed when I first marked Fr Iggy Clarke.' Fr Jim Stanley played for Kildare in the 1919 All-Ireland final under an assumed name, and Fr Seamus Hetherton lined out for Cavan in the 1952 decider. Other notable GAA clergy include Con Cotrell and Paddy Barry (both Cork); Ray Reidy (Tipperary); Liam and Séamus Ryan; the Fitzmaurice brothers, Willie and Paudie (both Limerick); Tommy Murphy (Kilkenny); and Kevin Connolly of Louth, footballer and champion athlete.

Several priests have also served as county managers in recent times, including Fr Michael O'Brien, Fr Liam Kelleher, Fr Harry Bohan and Fr Tom Fogarty, while Fr Seamus Gardiner is spokesman for the National Referees Association. Catholic schools run by priests or Christian Brothers also played a huge role in the development of players throughout the GAA's history. Institutions such as St Brendan's, Killarney; St Kieran's, Kilkenny; St Jarlath's, Tuam; St Colman's, Newry; and St Mel's, Longford were really

GAA academies, producing a lot of the Games' top stars. Societal changes, however, have seen the role of the Catholic school in the GAA diminish in recent years, with the club replacing it as the prime influence on a player's development.

– ROUGH JOURNEY –

Roy Keane once raged that the Irish soccer players were forced to sit in the 'cheap seats' on planes for away trips while FAI officials lounged in first class. Keane complained that by the time the travelling party reached their destination, some players were suffering from cramp due to the lack of legroom, thereby hindering preparations for the match.

Lucky, then, that Keane wasn't a member of the Dublin senior football team that played Kerry in the All-Ireland semi-final of 1941. The Dubs commuted by train to Tralee for the match, but along the way the engine ran out of fuel. Afraid of being late for their Kingdom date, some of the players were forced to disembark and chop down nearby trees so that the train could continue its journey. Later, the weary Dublin side were no match for Kerry, who went on to win that year's All-Ireland.

– KICKING SAM –

Some supporters take championship defeat worse than others. But back in 2002, one man in Galway took his frustration at the county's All-Ireland quarter-final exit at the hands of Kerry to a shockingly disgraceful level. As All-Ireland champions in 2001, the Sam Maguire Cup was still doing the rounds in Galway, and the week after their defeat to Kerry, Sam was on a tour of pubs in Tuam. However, one man managed to seize the cup and make off with it, horrifying onlookers as he kicked the cup for twenty yards down Shop Street in the middle of the town. Luckily, there was only slight damage done to the cup, and while Gardaí said they were aware of the incident, no formal proceedings were initiated as there had been no official complaint. Sam was reunited with Croke Park soon afterwards, and Armagh gave it a safe home for the following 12 months.

– MEDALS OF HONOUR –

As far as multiple All-Ireland medal winners go, Kerry footballers are in a league of their own. Five of Mick O'Dwyer's Kerry team of the 1970s and '80s – Ogie Moran, Páidí Ó Sé, Pat Spillane, Ger Power and Mikey Sheehy – hold eight All-Ireland medals each, while another five Kerrymen have seven – Dan O'Keeffe, John O'Keeffe, Jack O'Shea, Charlie Nelligan, Seán Walsh and Mick Spillane.

Legendary Cork hurler Christy Ring also has eight medals, along with Tipp hurler John Doyle and Kilkenny's Frank Cummins, but it is Cummins's long-time teammate Noel Skehan who heads the overall list. The enduring Kilkenny goalkeeper won a remarkable nine Celtic Crosses between 1963 and '83, although three of those were as a sub, unlike Doyle and Ring, who both bagged their total haul on the field of play.

Next up on the winners chart is a quartet of glorious Cats from the early years of the GAA. Jack Rockford, Dick Walsh, Sim Walton and Dick Doyle all won seven All-Irelands with Kilkenny between 1904 and 1913, while Tipp's Jimmy Doyle, a namesake of his teammate John, won six between 1958 and '71, and Eddie Keher of Kilkenny won six between 1963 and '75. Four of the dominant Kilkenny team of the 2000s – Michael Kavanagh, Henry Shefflin, Noel Hickey and Eddie Brennan – have half a dozen medals trousered already and are closing in rapidly on Ring's and Doyle's record. Cork great Jimmy Barry-Murphy has an unusual collection of six All-Ireland medals: five in hurling and one in football.

– THE TAILTEANN GAMES –

The original Tailteann Games – a sporting festival held in honour of the ancient Queen Tailtiu – were last staged around 1180 AD, when the Norman Invasion put an end to the tradition, but the GAA decided to revive the series in 1921 when Eamon de Valera announced a new 'meeting of the Irish Race'. However, due to the Civil War, the games were not held for a further three years, until 1924. The events, which were staged in Croke Park, were rekindled, and amateurs of Irish birth or extraction were entitled to compete. Athletes from Australia, Britain, Canada, Newfoundland, New Zealand, South Africa and the USA made the journey to compete, and the GAA actually built the Hogan Stand to mark the 1924 games. The Tailteann Games were held again in 1928 and '32, but as interest dwindled, the GAA decided to end the series. The sports contested at the Tailteann Games were athletics, boxing, camogie, cycling, fencing, football, gymnastics, handball, hurling, motor racing, rising and striking the hurling ball, road bowls, rounders, shooting, swimming and yachting.

– LONGEST-SERVING MANAGERS –

The attrition rate among GAA managers in football and hurling is now as high as most professional sports. And just like the pro game, managerial tenure can only be secured through success. Having taken over in 2002, Tyrone manager Mickey Harte is the longest-serving football manager, closely followed by Monaghan's Seamus McEnaney, who took charge in 2004, as did Waterford's John Kiely. Harte's longevity is obviously bolstered by the three All-Irelands he has won, although he still came under pressure early in the 2008 championship after his side lost to Down in Ulster. Kerry's Jack O'Connor is back for a second spell with the county after spending three years in charge, while John O'Mahony is also back with his native county for a second turn after managing Leitrim and Galway in the interim.

In hurling, Brian Cody stands apart after assuming the Kilkenny manager's position in 1998. After Gerald McCarthy was forced to resign as Cork manager after three years, it means that next in line after Cody in terms of longevity are Antrim's joint managers, Terence 'Sambo' McNaughton and Dominic McKinley, who have had three years in charge of the Saffrons. Gerald McCarthy and

Justin McCarthy, now at the helm in Limerick, have been around the block in terms of management, with Justin spending seven years in charge of Waterford, a team previously managed by Gerald for five years. However, the father figure of management is Mick O'Dwyer, now in charge of his fourth county, having led the great Kerry team between 1975 and '89, Kildare (twice: from 1991 to '94 and from 1997 to 2002), Laois (from 2002 to '06) and now Wicklow (2006 to present). In total, O'Dwyer has spent 32 years in intercounty management.

CURRENT MANAGERS WHO HAVE SERVED FOR OVER TWO YEARS

FOOTBALL	COUNTY	APPOINTED
Mickey Harte	Tyrone	November 2002
Seamus McEnaney	Monaghan	October 2004
John Kiely	Waterford	December 2004
Eamon McEneaney	Louth	November 2005
Tomás Ó Flatharta	Westmeath	November 2005
Mickey Ned O'Sullivan	Limerick	October 2005
John O'Mahony	Mayo	November 2006
Mick O'Dwyer	Wicklow	October 2006
HURLING	**COUNTY**	**APPOINTED**
Brian Cody	Kilkenny	November 1998
Terence McNaughton	Antrim	November 2006
Dominic McKinley	Antrim	November 2006

– DEAD RUBBER –

A few recent All-Ireland finals have been, metaphorically speaking, 'over before they started', though none can better the 1911 hurling decider for one-sidedness. Limerick refused to play the clash against Kilkenny in Thurles after the original match set for Cork was postponed because of the bad playing surface. Kilkenny were awarded the title by the powers that be, though a showpiece was hastily arranged anyway, with Tipperary playing the Cats solely for bragging rights. Tipperary had themselves, however, been the beneficiaries of a hectic competition previously. In 1899, they were awarded the title when the competition was left unfinished, while two of Cork's thirty All-Ireland hurling titles (in 1890 and 1892) came in similar circumstances. And to this day, no team can claim to have won the 1888 All-Ireland hurling title, after the competition was abandoned. The reason? Many of the GAA's top brass and best athletes embarked on the 'Invasion' tour of America and arrived back just in time for the 1889 competition to commence.

– NOT ALL-WHITE ON THE NIGHT –

The great Down football team of the 1960s were one of the first counties to break with an old GAA custom, the wearing of white shorts. Until then, county sides wore their homeland coloured jerseys, but the togs remained pure, so to speak. Not content were they with upsetting the natural order of things on the pitch by beating the likes of Kerry (1960 and 1968) and Offaly (1961) in All-Ireland finals, they also started sporting black shorts with their red-and-black trimmed jerseys as they became the first Ulster county to win Sam Maguire on three occasions in one decade. The subject of coloured shorts came to the fore again in 1974 when Dublin changed from their traditional light-blue shirts with white togs to the now instantly recognisable sky-blue-and-navy strip.

According to Dublin GAA folklore, one progressive young county board employee deemed the old gear dreary when viewed on television and lobbied for change. Incidentally, Dublin went on later that year to end an 11-year famine and bring Sam Maguire back to the capital.

– FIGHTING TALK –

In 2005, the GAA unveiled their latest match-day facility in the bowels of Croke Park – a brand-new media room. Little did they know, however, that the plush new room would be subject to such a fiery maiden voyage. The occasion, of course, was the 2005 International Rules Series between Ireland and Australia – or the 'ill-fated second Test', to give it its eventual title. Within seconds of the start of the game, Graham Geraghty was concussed under a hefty challenge from an opponent, and the opening two quarters of the game were marred with sporadic outbreaks of violence as the match turned to farce. Eventually, Australia won the Test – and the Series – but the best action was still to come.

First, Ireland manager Seán Boylan entered the media room, flanked by captain Kieran McGeeney. The Meath native revealed, first, that the Irish camp had been warned that Geraghty would be targeted by the Australians, and then that he had contemplated taking his players off the pitch. McGeeney, though, was typically direct in his summation. 'If you want to box, say you want to box; put on your gloves or go bare-knuckle,' said the Armagh man. 'It doesn't take a brave man to elbow somebody in the face ... if somebody grabs you by the neck, what are you going to do? Say "Sorry, excuse me, you're not allowed to do that." "Oh darn, dash, I think I'll stop here," when somebody elbows you in your kidney. Ireland is full of boys that love to fight, full of them . . . But if you want to fight, say you want to fight.'

If that wasn't juicy enough for the assembled media, outspoken Aussie boss Kevin Sheedy's assertions that 'Ireland were the aggressors last week and this week' was followed with a direct hit at the Irish press. Asked if he felt the Series had a future, Sheedy blasted: 'Every time Australia win, the Series is coming to an end. Unbelievable! You're the greatest conmen I've ever met.'

– KILKENNY HURLERS DO NOT TRAVEL WELL! –

Most teams engaged in All-Ireland finals travel to Dublin (or wherever the final might be scheduled for) on the evening prior to the match. Kilkenny more or less abided by that custom for a long number of years but never since 1966.

They had a team of stars that year and qualified for the All-Ireland final with Cork. The Rebels had been without an All-Ireland title for 12 years by then and did not have a single All-Ireland medal-holder on the side. Naturally the Cats were strong favourites but, as sometimes happens, Cork exceptionally played well and brought home the Liam MacCarthy Cup.

But there was a sequel in the form of a story that the Kilkenny hurlers were given sleeping pills on Saturday night in the hope that they would get a good night's rest in the hotel. They may have got that, but there was a faint feeling that maybe the effects of the tablets did not wear off until late afternoon on the Sunday and that it could have affected the course of play somewhat. One never knows, but Kilkenny have slept in their own beds at home prior to every final since then. And they have not done badly under the new system – 17 All-Ireland titles (at the time of going to press) in 32 years as against 15 in the preceding 79 years of championships.

There's no place like home!

– SNAP HAPPY –

The media is often treated with a mixture of suspicion and paranoia by intercounty managers and players, though its defence remains that no newspaper, television channel, website, radio programme or reporter ever won or lost a team an All-Ireland. That may be true, but Down could be forgiven for cursing a pair of photographers who lingered a little too long on the pitch at the start of the 1960 All-Ireland football final. The snappers were doing their usual throw-in shots, but just as Tadhg Lyne fielded the ball, he barged his way into the two cameramen, and the referee, to the great bemusement of the Down squad, awarded a free to Kerry. Luckily for the photographers, Down won anyway and their 'foul' hadn't affected the result.

– DRINK MONEY –

While Guinness sponsorship of the hurling championship is still a source of some angst for certain members of the GAA, alcoholic endorsements of our national games are nothing new. John 'Kerry' O'Donnell, the legendary GAA activist in New York and saviour of Gaelic Park in the Bronx, enticed beer companies to sponsor tournaments stateside between the 1930s and the '60s, and the money went to fund football and hurling tours around the globe in the 1960s.

– DOUBLE TOPS –

The first player to accomplish the rare honour of winning senior All-Ireland medals with two different counties was William J. Spain. He had a head start on everyone else by playing on the Limerick Commercials team that won the first ever All-Ireland football championship (1887) for Limerick. He followed up by playing on the Dublin team that won the hurling All-Ireland of 1889.

William Guiry of Limerick was not far behind, claiming an Ireland medal in football with Limerick in 1896 and another with Dublin a year later.

Next in order of seniority was Pierce Grace of Kilkenny with a veritable haul of All-Ireland medals – two football ones with Dublin (1906 and '07) and later three hurling medals with the Cats (1911, '12 and '13).

Garrett Howard won the first of five All-Ireland hurling medals playing for his native Limerick in 1921. He helped his county to two more titles (1934 and '36), but in-between he hurled with Dublin and won two All-Irelands with his adopted county (1924 and '27). The 1927 team was known as the 'Garda Team' as it contained many members of the force who happened by design or otherwise to be stationed in Dublin at the time. One such member was Mattie Power of Kilkenny, who won four All-Irelands with his home county (1922, '32. '33 and '35) in addition to the Dublin one with that 'Garda team' of 1927.

Mick Gill of Galway has the distinction of winning All-Ireland medals with different counties in the shortest period of time. On 14 September 1924 he was a member of the Galway hurling team that beat Limerick in the final of the 1923 championship; three months later, on December 14, he was a member of the Dublin team that won the All-Ireland of that year by beating Galway in the final!

By then, Larry Stanley of Kildare had achieved the football double – he captained Kildare to win the All-Ireland of 1919 (versus Galway), and four year later was on the Dublin team that beat Kerry in the final.

Jack Flavin of Kerry played at right half-forward for the Kingdom when they won the All-Ireland title of 1937; he occupied the same position on the Galway team that beat Kerry in the final of the following year. He was still wearing the number 10 when Galway lost to Kerry in the final of 1940. He played in the corner when Galway lost yet again in the final of 1942 – this time to Dublin.

And would you believe that Skerries man Bobby Beggs was on that Dublin side that opposed Flavin, even though they were teammates in 1938 when as 'Galway men' they beat Kerry. Bobby was a familiar figure in Croke Park on final day, having played for Dublin (against Galway) in the final of 1934 and for Galway in the finals of '38 (plus replay),'40 and '41 before transferring back home and lining out with the Dubs against Galway again in 1942. And he even played in the curtain-raiser before the Roscommon–Cavan final of 1943 – playing for his club Skerries Harps in a Dublin Championship game.

The case of these strange doubles keeps getting stranger: Caleb Crone, a Cork man, played for Dublin on that '42 team that won Sam and was the direct opponent of Flavin, the Kerryman playing for Galway. Then in 1945, Caleb was back in Cork and a member of the Rebel team that won the All-Ireland of that year when they beat the Bréifne side in the final.

We now come Oliver Gough, the last in time so far to have gained top honours with separate counties. He gained an All-Ireland hurling medal with Wexford in 1955, coming on as a sub for the great Ned Wheeler in the final against Galway, and again in 1963 when coming on as a sub for Johnny McGovern of Kilkenny in the final against Waterford.

All in all, there is a fair spread of successful peripatetic Gaelic players.

– THE EVOLUTION OF THE LINE BALL IN GAELIC FOOTBALL –

What had Gaelic football, rugby and soccer in common in the early years? The answer is that the ball was thrown back and not kicked to restart play after the ball had crossed the sideline and was thus out of play. It has remained more or less the same in rugby and soccer ever since organised sport was 'decriminalised' in the second half of the nineteenth century following the repeal of a Statute Ban that had stretched back over 500 years. The throw-in lasted in Gaelic football until the championship of 1946; prior to that, all Gaelic football teams carried a good 'thrower' or two and 'throwing legends' existed. However, scores from throws were not allowed. A kick from the ground replaced the throw in 1946, but under the influence of the Aussie Rules, the sideline kick was changed from a ground one to a kick from the hands in 1990.

– SIBLING RIVALRY –

Jim Cronin of Milltown county Kerry was full-forward on the Cork team that won the All-Ireland of 1945, and his brother John, who had previously played with Cork, was centre-back on the successful Kerry teams of 1953 and '55 – football in all cases!

The Power brothers of Waterford did something similar to the Cronins, but in the great game of hurling, Séamus partnered Philly Grimes at midfield on the Waterford team that won the All-Ireland of 1959. A year later, his brother Seán came on as a sub for the late Séamus Quaid on the Wexford team that beat Tipp in a fine All-Ireland final.

We have already mentioned Pierce Grace of Kilkenny under another heading and he fits into this category as well; the Graces were a noted sporting family who among them amassed a total of 15 All-Ireland medals. The names of Dick, Jack and Pierce were famous in hurling and football lore in both Dublin and Kilkenny. Jack won five football crowns with Dublin and was captain on two occasions, and Dick was on the Kilkenny team that won the county's first All-Ireland in 1904 and added a few more later.

Around the World in GAA Days
Aaron Dunne

ISBN 9781845963637
£12.99 (paperback)

Available October 2009

From its humble beginnings in the lobby of a Thurles
hotel in the late nineteenth century, the GAA has grown to
become the biggest amateur sporting organisation in the
world, spreading its wings to all corners of the globe in the
process.

In *Around the World in GAA Days*, Aaron Dunne takes us
on a journey around the world documenting the spectacular
rise of Ireland's national games. From the Gulf Games of
the Dubai Celts in the Middle East to the development
of underage hurling in Singapore, from the week-long
Australian State Games to the rebirth of camogie Down
Under, and from the annual Canadian Gaelic Games festival
to the powerhouse GAA cities of Chicago, New York and
Boston in North America, Dunne has travelled around the
globe to meet the people who work tirelessly to promote and
maintain Gaelic Games on the international scene.

Containing all you ever wanted to know about the GAA
and its popularity abroad, *Around the World in GAA Days*
is a colourful and entertaining insight into the life of the
modern, and not so modern, Irish emigrant.

Travelling the Globe
with Gaelic Games from
Beijing to Bangkok and
New York to New South Wales

AARON
DUNNE

AROUND
THE WORLD IN
GAA DAYS

The GAA: An Oral History
John Scally

ISBN 9781845964436
£14.99 (paperback)

Available now

For more than 100 years, the GAA has been a fixed point in a fast-changing age. *The GAA: An Oral History* marks the 125th anniversary of the Association – as seen through the eyes of the key personalities who shaped it. They go behind the scenes and offer unique eyewitness accounts of the dramas on and off the pitch that captivated, enthralled and occasionally infuriated the nation.

More than 100 interviews with players and managers of the present and the past, such as Babs Keating, Jimmy Barry-Murphy, Ger Loughnane, D.J. Carey, Liam Griffin, Mick O'Dwyer, Colm O'Rourke, John O'Mahony, Joe Brolly and Matt Connor, are included. New light is shed on old controversies, fresh insights into the players and personalities that linger long in the memory are provided and the epic contests that turned the national games into the national soap opera are recounted by those who were there.

This celebration of the good, the bad and the beautiful of the GAA is a must for all sports fans.

THE
GAA
AN ORAL HISTORY

JOHN
SCALLY

Foreword by
JACK O'SHEA